Python Network Programming Cookbook

Over 70 detailed recipes to develop practical solutions for a wide range of real-world network programming tasks

Dr. M. O. Faruque Sarker

[PACKT] PUBLISHING
open source
community experience distilled

BIRMINGHAM - MUMBAI

Python Network Programming Cookbook

First published: March 2014

Production Reference: 1190314

Published by Packt Publishing Ltd.
Livery Place
35 Livery Street
Birmingham B3 2PB, UK.

ISBN 978-1-84951-346-3

www.packtpub.com

Cover Image by Gabrielay La Pintura (linaza100@hotmail.com)

Credits

Author
Dr. M. O. Faruque Sarker

Reviewers
Ahmed Soliman Farghal
Vishrut Mehta
Tom Stephens
Deepak Thukral

Acquisition Editors
Aarthi Kumarswamy
Owen Roberts

Content Development Editor
Arun Nadar

Technical Editors
Manan Badani
Shashank Desai

Copy Editors
Janbal Dharmaraj
Deepa Nambiar
Karuna Narayanan

Project Coordinator
Sanchita Mandal

Proofreaders
Faye Coulman
Paul Hindle
Joanna McMahon

Indexer
Mehreen Deshmukh

Production Coordinator
Nilesh R. Mohite

Cover Work
Nilesh R. Mohite

About the Author

Dr. M. O. Faruque Sarker is a software architect, and DevOps engineer who's currently working at University College London (UCL), United Kingdom. In recent years, he has been leading a number of Python software development projects, including the implementation of an interactive web-based scientific computing framework using the IPython Notebook service at UCL. He is a specialist and an expert in open source technologies, for example, e-learning and web application platforms, agile software development, and IT service management methodologies such as DSDM Atern and ITIL Service management frameworks.

Dr. Sarker received his PhD in multirobot systems from University of South Wales where he adopted various Python open source projects for integrating the complex software infrastructure of one of the biggest multirobot experiment testbeds in UK. To drive his multirobot fleet, he designed and implemented a decoupled software architecture called hybrid event-driven architecture on D-Bus. Since 1999, he has been deploying Linux and open source software in commercial companies, educational institutions, and multinational consultancies. He was invited to work on the Google Summer of Code 2009/2010 programs for contributing to the BlueZ and Tahoe-LAFS open source projects.

Currently, Dr. Sarker has a research interest in self-organized cloud architecture. In his spare time, he likes to play with his little daughter, Ayesha, and is keen to learn about child-centric educational methods that can empower children with self-confidence by engaging with their environment.

I would like to thank everyone who has contributed to the publication of this book, including the publisher, technical reviewers, editors, friends, and my family members, specially my wife Shahinur Rijuani for her love and support in my work. I also thank the readers who have patiently been waiting for this book and who have given me lots of valuable feedback.

About the Reviewers

Ahmed Soliman Farghal is an entrepreneur and software and systems engineer coming from a diverse background of highly scalable applications design, mission-critical systems, asynchronous data analytics, social networks design, reactive distributed systems, and systems administration and engineering. He has also published a technology patent in distributed computer-based virtual laboratories and designed numerous large-scale distributed systems for massive-scale enterprise customers.

A software engineer at heart, he is experienced in over 10 programming languages, but most recently, he is busy designing and writing applications in Python, Ruby, and Scala for several customers. He is also an open source evangelist and activist. He contributed and maintained several open source projects on the Web.

Ahmed is a co-founder of Cloud Niners Ltd., a software and services company focusing on highly scalable cloud-based applications that have been delivering private and public cloud computing services to customers in the MEA region on different platforms and technologies.

A quick acknowledgment to some of the people who changed my entire life for the better upon meeting or working with them; this gratitude does not come in a specific order but resembles a great appreciation for their support, help, and influence through my personal life and professional career.

I would also like to thank Prof. Dr. Soliman Farghal, my father, for his continuous help and support and giving me an opportunity to play with a real computer before I was able to speak properly and Sinar Shebl, my wife; she has been of great help and a deep source of inspiration.

Vishrut Mehta has been involved in open source development since two years and contributed to various organizations, such as Sahana Software Foundation, GNOME, and E-cidadania; he has participated in Google Summer of Code last year.

He is also the organization administrator for Google Code-In and has been actively involved in other open source programs.

He is a dual degree student at IIIT Hyderabad, and now he is pursuing his research under Dr. Vasudeva Varma on topics related to Cloud Computing, Distributed Systems, Big Data, and Software Defined Networks.

I would like to thank my advisors, Dr. Venkatesh Choppella and Dr. Vasudeva Varma, who showed me the direction in my work and helped me a lot.
I would also like to thank my Google Summer of Code mentor, Patirica Tressel.

Tom Stephens has worked in software development for nearly 10 years and is currently working in embedded development dealing with smartcards, cryptography, and RFID in the Denver metro area. His diverse background includes experience ranging from embedded virtual machines to web UX/UI design to enterprise Business Intelligence. He is most passionate about good software design, including intelligent testing and constantly evolving practices to produce a better product with minimal effort.

Deepak Thukral is a polyglot who is also a contributor to various open source Python projects. He moved from India to Europe where he worked for various companies helping them scale their platforms with Python.

www.PacktPub.com

Support files, eBooks, discount offers, and more

You might want to visit www.PacktPub.com for support files and downloads related to your book.

Did you know that Packt offers eBook versions of every book published, with PDF and ePub files available? You can upgrade to the eBook version at www.PacktPub.com and as a print book customer, you are entitled to a discount on the eBook copy. Get in touch with us at service@packtpub.com for more details.

At www.PacktPub.com, you can also read a collection of free technical articles, sign up for a range of free newsletters and receive exclusive discounts and offers on Packt books and eBooks.

PACKTLIB®

http://PacktLib.PacktPub.com

Do you need instant solutions to your IT questions? PacktLib is Packt's online digital book library. Here, you can access, read and search across Packt's entire library of books.

Why subscribe?

- Fully searchable across every book published by Packt
- Copy and paste, print and bookmark content
- On demand and accessible via web browser

Free access for Packt account holders

If you have an account with Packt at www.PacktPub.com, you can use this to access PacktLib today and view nine entirely free books. Simply use your login credentials for immediate access.

Table of Contents

Preface

All praises be to God! I am glad that this book is now published, and I would like to thank everyone behind the publication of this book. This book is an exploratory guide to network programming in Python. It has touched a wide range of networking protocols such as TCP/UDP, HTTP/HTTPS, FTP, SMTP, POP3, IMAP, CGI, and so forth. With the power and interactivity of Python, it brings joy and fun to develop various scripts for performing real-world tasks on network and system administration, web application development, interacting with your local and remote network, low-level network packet capture and analysis, and so on. The primary focus of this book is to give you a hands-on experience on the topics covered. So, this book covers less theory, but it's packed with practical materials.

This book is written with a "devops" mindset where a developer is also more or less in charge of operation, that is, deploying the application and managing various aspects of it, such as remote server administration, monitoring, scaling-up, and optimizing for better performance. This book introduces you to a bunch of open-source, third-party Python libraries, which are awesome to use in various usecases. I use many of these libraries on a daily basis to enjoy automating my devops tasks. For example, I use Fabric for automating software deployment tasks and other libraries for other purposes, such as, searching things on the Internet, screen-scraping, or sending an e-mail from a Python script.

I hope you'll enjoy the recipes presented in this book and extend them to make them even more powerful and enjoyable.

What this book covers

Chapter 1, Sockets, IPv4, and Simple Client/Server Programming, introduces you to Python's core networking library with various small tasks and enables you to create your first client-server application.

Chapter 2, Multiplexing Socket I/O for Better Performance, discusses various useful techniques for scaling your client/server applications with default and third-party libraries.

Chapter 3, IPv6, Unix Domain Sockets, and Network Interfaces, focuses more on administering your local machine and looking after your local area network.

Chapter 4, Programming with HTTP for the Internet, enables you to create a mini command-line browser with various features such as submitting web forms, handling cookies, managing partial downloads, compressing data, and serving secure contents over HTTPS.

Chapter 5, E-mail Protocols, FTP, and CGI Programming, brings you the joy of automating your FTP and e-mail tasks such as manipulating your Gmail account, and reading or sending e-mails from a script or creating a guest book for your web application.

Chapter 6, Screen-scraping and Other Practical Applications, introduces you to various third-party Python libraries that do some practical tasks, for example, locating companies on Google maps, grabbing information from Wikipedia, searching code repository on GitHub, or reading news from the BBC.

Chapter 7, Programming Across Machine Boundaries, gives you a taste of automating your system administration and deployment tasks over SSH. You can run commands, install packages, or set up new websites remotely from your laptop.

Chapter 8, Working with Web Services – XML-RPC, SOAP, and REST, introduces you to various API protocols such as XML-RPC, SOAP, and REST. You can programmatically ask any website or web service for information and interact with them. For example, you can search for products on Amazon or Google.

Chapter 9, Network Monitoring and Security, introduces you to various techniques for capturing, storing, analyzing, and manipulating network packets. This encourages you to go further to investigate your network security issues using concise Python scripts.

What you need for this book

You need a working PC or laptop, preferably with any modern Linux operating system such as Ubuntu, Debian, CentOS, and so on. Most of the recipes in this book will run on other platforms such as Windows and Mac OS.

You also need a working Internet connection to install the third-party software libraries mentioned with respective recipes. If you do not have an Internet connection, you can download those third-party libraries and install them in one go.

The following is a list of those third-party libraries with their download URLs:

- **ntplib**: `https://pypi.python.org/pypi/ntplib/`
- **diesel**: `https://pypi.python.org/pypi/diesel/`
- **nmap**: `https://pypi.python.org/pypi/python-nmap`
- **scapy**: `https://pypi.python.org/pypi/scapy`
- **netifaces**: `https://pypi.python.org/pypi/netifaces/`
- **netaddr**: `https://pypi.python.org/pypi/netaddr`
- **pyopenssl**: `https://pypi.python.org/pypi/pyOpenSSL`

- **pygeocoder**: `https://pypi.python.org/pypi/pygocoder`
- **pyyaml**: `https://pypi.python.org/pypi/PyYAML`
- **requests**: `https://pypi.python.org/pypi/requests`
- **feedparser**: `https://pypi.python.org/pypi/feedparser`
- **paramiko**: `https://pypi.python.org/pypi/paramiko/`
- **fabric**: `https://pypi.python.org/pypi/Fabric`
- **supervisor**: `https://pypi.python.org/pypi/supervisor`
- **xmlrpclib**: `https://pypi.python.org/pypi/xmlrpclib`
- **SOAPpy**: `https://pypi.python.org/pypi/SOAPpy`
- **bottlenose**: `https://pypi.python.org/pypi/bottlenose`
- **construct**: `https://pypi.python.org/pypi/construct/`

The non-Python software needed to run some recipes are as follows:

- **postfix**: `http://www.postfix.org/`
- **openssh server**: `http://www.openssh.com/`
- **mysql server**: `http://downloads.mysql.com/`
- **apache2**: `http://httpd.apache.org/download.cgi`

Who this book is for

If you are a network programmer, system/network administrator, or a web application developer, this book is ideal for you. You should have a basic familiarity with the Python programming language and TCP/IP networking concepts. However, if you are a novice, you will develop an understanding of the concepts as you progress with this book. This book will serve as supplementary material for developing hands-on skills in any academic course on network programming.

Conventions

In this book, you will find a number of styles of text that distinguish between different kinds of information. Here are some examples of these styles and an explanation of their meaning.

Code words in text, database table names, folder names, filenames, file extensions, pathnames, dummy URLs, user input, and Twitter handles are shown as follows:

If you need to know the IP address of a remote machine you can use the built-in library function `gethostbyname()`.

A block of code is set as follows:

```
def test_socket_timeout():
    s = socket.socket(socket.AF_INET, socket.SOCK_STREAM)
    print "Default socket timeout: %s" %s.gettimeout()
    s.settimeout(100)
    print "Current socket timeout: %s" %s.gettimeout()
```

Any command-line input or output is written as follows:

```
$ python 2_5_echo_server_with_diesel.py --port=8800
[2013/04/08 11:48:32] {diesel} WARNING:Starting diesel <hand-rolled
 select.epoll>
```

New terms and **important words** are shown in bold.

> Warnings or important notes appear in a box like this.

> Tips and tricks appear like this.

Reader feedback

Feedback from our readers is always welcome. Let us know what you think about this book—what you liked or may have disliked. Reader feedback is important for us to develop titles that you really get the most out of.

To send us general feedback, simply send an e-mail to `feedback@packtpub.com`, and mention the book title via the subject of your message.

If there is a topic that you have expertise in and you are interested in either writing or contributing to a book, see our author guide on `www.packtpub.com/authors`.

Customer support

Now that you are the proud owner of a Packt book, we have a number of things to help you to get the most from your purchase.

Downloading the example code

You can download the example code files for all Packt books you have purchased from your account at `http://www.packtpub.com`. If you purchased this book elsewhere, you can visit `http://www.packtpub.com/support` and register to have the files e-mailed directly to you.

Errata

Although we have taken every care to ensure the accuracy of our content, mistakes do happen. If you find a mistake in one of our books—maybe a mistake in the text or the code—we would be grateful if you would report this to us. By doing so, you can save other readers from frustration and help us improve subsequent versions of this book. If you find any errata, please report them by visiting `http://www.packtpub.com/submit-errata`, selecting your book, clicking on the **errata submission form** link, and entering the details of your errata. Once your errata are verified, your submission will be accepted and the errata will be uploaded on our website, or added to any list of existing errata, under the Errata section of that title. Any existing errata can be viewed by selecting your title from `http://www.packtpub.com/support`.

Piracy

Piracy of copyright material on the Internet is an ongoing problem across all media. At Packt, we take the protection of our copyright and licenses very seriously. If you come across any illegal copies of our works, in any form, on the Internet, please provide us with the location address or website name immediately so that we can pursue a remedy.

Please contact us at `copyright@packtpub.com` with a link to the suspected pirated material.

We appreciate your help in protecting our authors, and our ability to bring you valuable content.

Questions

You can contact us at `questions@packtpub.com` if you are having a problem with any aspect of the book, and we will do our best to address it.

1

Sockets, IPv4, and Simple Client/Server Programming

In this chapter, we will cover the following recipes:

- Printing your machine's name and IPv4 address
- Retrieving a remote machine's IP address
- Converting an IPv4 address to different formats
- Finding a service name, given the port and protocol
- Converting integers to and from host to network byte order
- Setting and getting the default socket timeout
- Handling socket errors gracefully
- Modifying a socket's send/receive buffer size
- Changing a socket to the blocking/non-blocking mode
- Reusing socket addresses
- Printing the current time from the Internet time server
- Writing a SNTP client
- Writing a simple echo client/server application

Introduction

This chapter introduces Python's core networking library through some simple recipes. Python's `socket` module has both class-based and instances-based utilities. The difference between a class-based and instance-based method is that the former doesn't need an instance of a socket object. This is a very intuitive approach. For example, in order to print your machine's IP address, you don't need a socket object. Instead, you can just call the socket's class-based methods. On the other hand, if you need to send some data to a server application, it is more intuitive that you create a socket object to perform that explicit operation. The recipes presented in this chapter can be categorized into three groups as follows:

- In the first few recipes, the class-based utilities have been used in order to extract some useful information about host, network, and any target service.
- After that, some more recipes have been presented using the instance-based utilities. Some common socket tasks, including manipulating the socket timeout, buffer size, blocking mode, and so on, have been demonstrated.
- Finally, both class-based and instance-based utilities have been used to construct some clients, which perform some practical tasks, for example, synchronizing the machine time with an Internet server or writing a generic client/server script.

You can use these demonstrated approaches to write your own client/server application.

Printing your machine's name and IPv4 address

Sometimes, you need to quickly discover some information about your machine, for example, the host name, IP address, number of network interfaces, and so on. This is very easy to achieve using Python scripts.

Getting ready

You need to install Python on your machine before you start coding. Python comes preinstalled in most of the Linux distributions. For Microsoft Windows operating system, you can download binaries from the Python website: `http://www.python.org/download/`

You may consult the documentation of your OS to check and review your Python setup. After installing Python on your machine, you can try opening the Python interpreter from the command line by typing `python`. This will show the interpreter prompt, `>>>`, which should be similar to the following output:

```
~$ python
Python 2.7.1+ (r271:86832, Apr 11 2011, 18:05:24)
[GCC 4.5.2] on linux2
Type "help", "copyright", "credits" or "license" for more information. >>>
```

How to do it...

As this recipe is very short, you can try this in the Python interpreter interactively.

First, we need to import the Python `socket` library with the following command:

```
>>> import socket
```

Then, we call the `gethostname()` method from the `socket` library and store the result in a variable as follows:

```
>>> host_name = socket.gethostname()
>>> print "Host name: %s" %host_name
Host name: debian6
>>> print "IP address: %s" %socket.gethostbyname(host_name)
IP address: 127.0.1.1
```

The entire activity can be wrapped in a free-standing function, `print_machine_info()`, which uses the built-in socket class methods.

We call our function from the usual Python `__main__` block. During runtime, Python assigns values to some internal variables such as `__name__`. In this case, `__name__` refers to the name of the calling process. When running this script from the command line, as shown in the following command, the name will be `__main__`, but it will be different if the module is imported from another script. This means that when the module is called from the command line, it will automatically run our `print_machine_info` function; however, when imported separately, the user will need to explicitly call the function.

Listing 1.1 shows how to get our machine info, as follows:

```
#!/usr/bin/env python
# Python Network Programming Cookbook -- Chapter -1
# This program is optimized for Python 2.7. It may run on any
# other Python version with/without modifications.

import socket

def print_machine_info():
    host_name = socket.gethostname()
    ip_address = socket.gethostbyname(host_name)
    print "Host name: %s" % host_name
    print "IP address: %s" % ip_address

if __name__ == '__main__':
    print_machine_info()
```

In order to run this recipe, you can use the provided source file from the command line as follows:

```
$ python 1_1_local_machine_info.py
```

On my machine, the following output is shown:

```
Host name: debian6
IP address: 127.0.0.1
```

This output will be different on your machine depending on the system's host configuration.

How it works...

The import socket statement imports one of Python's core networking libraries. Then, we use the two utility functions, `gethostname()` and `gethostbyname(host_name)`. You can type `help(socket.gethostname)` to see the online help information from within the command line. Alternately, you can type the following address in your web browser at `http://docs.python.org/3/library/socket.html`. You can refer to the following command:

```
gethostname(...)
    gethostname() -> string
    Return the current host name.

gethostbyname(...)
   gethostbyname(host) -> address
    Return the IP address (a string of the form '255.255.255.255') for a host.
```

The first function takes no parameter and returns the current or localhost name. The second function takes a single `hostname` parameter and returns its IP address.

Retrieving a remote machine's IP address

Sometimes, you need to translate a machine's hostname into its corresponding IP address, for example, a quick domain name lookup. This recipe introduces a simple function to do that.

How to do it...

If you need to know the IP address of a remote machine, you can use a built-in library function, `gethostbyname()`. In this case, you need to pass the remote hostname as its parameter.

In this case, we need to call the `gethostbyname()` class function. Let's have a look inside this short code snippet.

Listing 1.2 shows how to get a remote machine's IP address as follows:

```
#!/usr/bin/env python
# Python Network Programming Cookbook -- Chapter - 1
# This program is optimized for Python 2.7.
# It may run on any other version with/without modifications.

import socket

def get_remote_machine_info():
    remote_host = 'www.python.org'
    try:
        print "IP address: %s" %socket.gethostbyname(remote_host)
    except socket.error, err_msg:
        print "%s: %s" %(remote_host, err_msg)

if __name__ == '__main__':
    get_remote_machine_info()
```

If you run the preceding code it gives the following output:

```
$ python 1_2_remote_machine_info.py
IP address of www.python.org: 82.94.164.162
```

How it works...

This recipe wraps the `gethostbyname()` method inside a user-defined function called `get_remote_machine_info()`. In this recipe, we introduced the notion of exception handling. As you can see, we wrapped the main function call inside a `try-except` block. This means that if some error occurs during the execution of this function, this error will be dealt with by this `try-except` block.

For example, let's change the `remote_host` value and replace `www.python.org` with something non-existent, for example, `www.pytgo.org`. Now run the following command:

```
$ python 1_2_remote_machine_info.py
www.pytgo.org: [Errno -5] No address associated with hostname
```

The `try-except` block catches the error and shows the user an error message that there is no IP address associated with the hostname, `www.pytgo.org`.

Converting an IPv4 address to different formats

When you would like to deal with low-level network functions, sometimes, the usual string notation of IP addresses are not very useful. They need to be converted to the packed 32-bit binary formats.

How to do it...

The Python socket library has utilities to deal with the various IP address formats. Here, we will use two of them: `inet_aton()` and `inet_ntoa()`.

Let us create the `convert_ip4_address()` function, where `inet_aton()` and `inet_ntoa()` will be used for the IP address conversion. We will use two sample IP addresses, `127.0.0.1` and `192.168.0.1`.

Listing 1.3 shows `ip4_address_conversion` as follows:

```
#!/usr/bin/env python
# Python Network Programming Cookbook -- Chapter - 1
# This program is optimized for Python 2.7.
# It may run on any other version with/without modifications.

import socket
from binascii import hexlify

def convert_ip4_address():
    for ip_addr in ['127.0.0.1', '192.168.0.1']:
        packed_ip_addr = socket.inet_aton(ip_addr)
        unpacked_ip_addr = socket.inet_ntoa(packed_ip_addr)
        print "IP Address: %s => Packed: %s, Unpacked: %s"\
     %(ip_addr, hexlify(packed_ip_addr), unpacked_ip_addr)

if __name__ == '__main__':
    convert_ip4_address()
```

Now, if you run this recipe, you will see the following output:

```
$ python 1_3_ip4_address_conversion.py

IP Address: 127.0.0.1 => Packed: 7f000001, Unpacked: 127.0.0.1
IP Address: 192.168.0.1 => Packed: c0a80001, Unpacked: 192.168.0.1
```

How it works...

In this recipe, the two IP addresses have been converted from a string to a 32-bit packed format using a `for-in` statement. Additionally, the Python `hexlify` function is called from the `binascii` module. This helps to represent the binary data in a hexadecimal format.

Finding a service name, given the port and protocol

If you would like to discover network services, it may be helpful to determine what network services run on which ports using either the TCP or UDP protocol.

Getting ready

If you know the port number of a network service, you can find the service name using the `getservbyport()` socket class function from the socket library. You can optionally give the protocol name when calling this function.

How to do it...

Let us define a `find_service_name()` function, where the `getservbyport()` socket class function will be called with a few ports, for example, `80, 25`. We can use Python's `for-in` loop construct.

Listing 1.4 shows `finding_service_name` as follows:

```
#!/usr/bin/env python
# Python Network Programming Cookbook -- Chapter - 1
# This program is optimized for Python 2.7.
# It may run on any other version with/without modifications.

import socket

def find_service_name():
    protocolname = 'tcp'
    for port in [80, 25]:
        print "Port: %s => service name: %s" %(port, socket.
getservbyport(port, protocolname))
    print "Port: %s => service name: %s" %(53, socket.
getservbyport(53, 'udp'))

if __name__ == '__main__':
    find_service_name()
```

If you run this script, you will see the following output:

```
$ python 1_4_finding_service_name.py

Port: 80 => service name: http
Port: 25 => service name: smtp
Port: 53 => service name: domain
```

How it works...

In this recipe, `for-in` statement is used to iterate over a sequence of variables. So for each iteration we use one IP address to convert them in their packed and unpacked format.

Converting integers to and from host to network byte order

If you ever need to write a low-level network application, it may be necessary to handle the low-level data transmission over the wire between two machines. This operation requires some sort of conversion of data from the native host operating system to the network format and vice versa. This is because each one has its own specific representation of data.

How to do it...

Python's socket library has utilities for converting from a network byte order to host byte order and vice versa. You may want to become familiar with them, for example, `ntohl()/htonl()`.

Let us define the `convert_integer()` function, where the `ntohl()/htonl()` socket class functions are used to convert IP address formats.

Listing 1.5 shows `integer_conversion` as follows:

```
#!/usr/bin/env python
# Python Network Programming Cookbook -- Chapter -
# This program is optimized for Python 2.7.
# It may run on any other version with/without modifications.
import socket
def convert_integer():
    data = 1234
    # 32-bit
    print "Original: %s => Long  host byte order: %s, Network byte
order: %s"\
    %(data, socket.ntohl(data), socket.htonl(data))
    # 16-bit
```

```
        print "Original: %s => Short  host byte order: %s, Network byte 
    order: %s"\
        %(data, socket.ntohs(data), socket.htons(data))
    if __name__ == '__main__':
        convert_integer()
```

If you run this recipe, you will see the following output:

```
$ python 1_5_integer_conversion.py 
Original: 1234 => Long  host byte order: 3523477504, Network byte order: 
3523477504
Original: 1234 => Short  host byte order: 53764, Network byte order: 53764
```

How it works...

Here, we take an integer and show how to convert it between network and host byte orders. The `ntohl()` socket class function converts from the network byte order to host byte order in a long format. Here, `n` represents network and `h` represents host; `l` represents long and `s` represents short, that is 16-bit.

Setting and getting the default socket timeout

Sometimes, you need to manipulate the default values of certain properties of a socket library, for example, the socket timeout.

How to do it...

You can make an instance of a socket object and call a `gettimeout()` method to get the default timeout value and the `settimeout()` method to set a specific timeout value. This is very useful in developing custom server applications.

We first create a socket object inside a `test_socket_timeout()` function. Then, we can use the getter/setter instance methods to manipulate timeout values.

Listing 1.6 shows `socket_timeout` as follows:

```
#!/usr/bin/env python
# Python Network Programming Cookbook -- Chapter - 1
# This program is optimized for Python 2.7. It may run on any
# other Python version with/without modifications

import socket
```

```
def test_socket_timeout():
    s = socket.socket(socket.AF_INET, socket.SOCK_STREAM)
    print "Default socket timeout: %s" %s.gettimeout()
    s.settimeout(100)
    print "Current socket timeout: %s" %s.gettimeout()

if __name__ == '__main__':
    test_socket_timeout()
```

After running the preceding script, you can see how this modifies the default socket timeout as follows:

```
$ python 1_6_socket_timeout.py
Default socket timeout: None
Current socket timeout: 100.0
```

How it works...

In this code snippet, we have first created a socket object by passing the socket family and socket type as the first and second arguments of the socket constructor. Then, you can get the socket timeout value by calling `gettimeout()` and alter the value by calling the `settimeout()` method. The timeout value passed to the `settimeout()` method can be in seconds (non-negative float) or `None`. This method is used for manipulating the blocking-socket operations. Setting a timeout of `None` disables timeouts on socket operations.

Handling socket errors gracefully

In any networking application, it is very common that one end is trying to connect, but the other party is not responding due to networking media failure or any other reason. The Python socket library has an elegant method of handing these errors via the `socket.error` exceptions. In this recipe, a few examples are presented.

How to do it...

Let us create a few try-except code blocks and put one potential error type in each block. In order to get a user input, the `argparse` module can be used. This module is more powerful than simply parsing command-line arguments using `sys.argv`. In the try-except blocks, put typical socket operations, for example, create a socket object, connect to a server, send data, and wait for a reply.

The following recipe illustrates the concepts in a few lines of code.

Listing 1.7 shows `socket_errors` as follows:

```
#!/usr/bin/env python
# Python Network Programming Cookbook -- Chapter - 1
# This program is optimized for Python 2.7. It may run on any
# other Python version with/without modifications.

import sys
import socket
import argparse


def main():
    # setup argument parsing
    parser = argparse.ArgumentParser(description='Socket Error
Examples')
    parser.add_argument('--host', action="store", dest="host",
required=False)
    parser.add_argument('--port', action="store", dest="port",
type=int, required=False)
    parser.add_argument('--file', action="store", dest="file",
required=False)
    given_args = parser.parse_args()
    host = given_args.host
    port = given_args.port
    filename = given_args.file

    # First try-except block -- create socket
    try:
        s = socket.socket(socket.AF_INET, socket.SOCK_STREAM)
    except socket.error, e:
        print "Error creating socket: %s" % e
        sys.exit(1)

    # Second try-except block -- connect to given host/port
    try:
        s.connect((host, port))
    except socket.gaierror, e:
        print "Address-related error connecting to server: %s" % e
        sys.exit(1)
    except socket.error, e:
        print "Connection error: %s" % e
        sys.exit(1)
```

```
    # Third try-except block -- sending data
    try:
        s.sendall("GET %s HTTP/1.0\r\n\r\n" % filename)
    except socket.error, e:
        print "Error sending data: %s" % e
        sys.exit(1)

    while 1:
        # Fourth tr-except block -- waiting to receive data from 
remote host
        try:
            buf = s.recv(2048)
        except socket.error, e:
            print "Error receiving data: %s" % e
            sys.exit(1)
        if not len(buf):
            break
        # write the received data
        sys.stdout.write(buf)

if __name__ == '__main__':
    main()
```

How it works...

In Python, passing command-line arguments to a script and parsing them in the script can be done using the `argparse` module. This is available in Python 2.7. For earlier versions of Python, this module is available separately in **Python Package Index** (**PyPI**). You can install this via `easy_install` or `pip`.

In this recipe, three arguments are set up: a hostname, port number, and filename. The usage of this script is as follows:

```
$ python 1_7_socket_errors.py –host=<HOST> --port=<PORT> --file=<FILE>
```

If you try with a non-existent host, this script will print an address error as follows:

```
$ python 1_7_socket_errors.py --host=www.pytgo.org --port=8080 
--file=1_7_socket_errors.py
Address-related error connecting to server: [Errno -5] No address 
associated with hostname
```

If there is no service on a specific port and if you try to connect to that port, then this will throw a connection timeout error as follows:

```
$ python 1_7_socket_errors.py --host=www.python.org --port=8080
--file=1_7_socket_errors.py
```

This will return the following error since the host, `www.python.org`, is not listening on port 8080:

```
Connection error: [Errno 110] Connection timed out
```

However, if you send an arbitrary request to a correct request to a correct port, the error may not be caught in the application level. For example, running the following script returns no error, but the HTML output tells us what's wrong with this script:

```
$ python 1_7_socket_errors.py --host=www.python.org --port=80 --file=1_7_
socket_errors.py


HTTP/1.1 404 Not found
Server: Varnish
Retry-After: 0
content-type: text/html
Content-Length: 77
Accept-Ranges: bytes
Date: Thu, 20 Feb 2014 12:14:01 GMT
Via: 1.1 varnish
Age: 0
Connection: close


<html>
<head>
<title> </title>
</head>
<body>
unknown domain: </body></html>
```

In the preceding example, four try-except blocks have been used. All blocks use `socket.error` except the second block, which uses `socket.gaierror`. This is used for address-related errors. There are two other types of exceptions: `socket.herror` is used for legacy C API, and if you use the `settimeout()` method in a socket, `socket.timeout` will be raised when a timeout occurs on that socket.

Modifying socket's send/receive buffer sizes

The default socket buffer size may not be suitable in many circumstances. In such circumstances, you can change the default socket buffer size to a more suitable value.

How to do it...

Let us manipulate the default socket buffer size using a socket object's `setsockopt()` method.

First, define two constants: `SEND_BUF_SIZE`/`RECV_BUF_SIZE` and then wrap a socket instance's call to the `setsockopt()` method in a function. It is also a good idea to check the value of the buffer size before modifying it. Note that we need to set up the send and receive buffer size separately.

Listing 1.8 shows how to modify socket send/receive buffer sizes as follows:

```
#!/usr/bin/env python
# Python Network Programming Cookbook -- Chapter - 1
# This program is optimized for Python 2.7. It may run on any
# other Python version with/without modifications

import socket

SEND_BUF_SIZE = 4096
RECV_BUF_SIZE = 4096

def modify_buff_size():
    sock = socket.socket(socket.AF_INET, socket.SOCK_STREAM )

    # Get the size of the socket's send buffer
    bufsize = sock.getsockopt(socket.SOL_SOCKET, socket.SO_SNDBUF)
    print "Buffer size [Before]:%d" %bufsize

    sock.setsockopt(socket.SOL_TCP, socket.TCP_NODELAY, 1)
    sock.setsockopt(
            socket.SOL_SOCKET,
            socket.SO_SNDBUF,
            SEND_BUF_SIZE)
    sock.setsockopt(
            socket.SOL_SOCKET,
            socket.SO_RCVBUF,
            RECV_BUF_SIZE)
```

```
        bufsize = sock.getsockopt(socket.SOL_SOCKET, socket.SO_SNDBUF)
        print "Buffer size [After]:%d" %bufsize

    if __name__ == '__main__':
        modify_buff_size()
```

If you run the preceding script, it will show the changes in the socket's buffer size. The following output may be different on your machine depending on your operating system's local settings:

```
$ python 1_8_modify_buff_size.py
Buffer size [Before]:16384
Buffer size [After]:8192
```

How it works...

You can call the `getsockopt()` and `setsockopt()` methods on a socket object to retrieve and modify the socket object's properties respectively. The `setsockopt()` method takes three arguments: `level`, `optname`, and `value`. Here, `optname` takes the option name and `value` is the corresponding value of that option. For the first argument, the needed symbolic constants can be found in the socket module (`SO_*etc.`).

Changing a socket to the blocking/non-blocking mode

By default, TCP sockets are placed in a blocking mode. This means the control is not returned to your program until some specific operation is complete. For example, if you call the `connect()` API, the connection blocks your program until the operation is complete. On many occasions, you don't want to keep your program waiting forever, either for a response from the server or for any error to stop the operation. For example, when you write a web browser client that connects to a web server, you should consider a stop functionality that can cancel the connection process in the middle of this operation. This can be achieved by placing the socket in the non-blocking mode.

How to do it...

Let us see what options are available under Python. In Python, a socket can be placed in the blocking or non-blocking mode. In the non-blocking mode, if any call to API, for example, `send()` or `recv()`, encounters any problem, an error will be raised. However, in the blocking mode, this will not stop the operation. We can create a normal TCP socket and experiment with both the blocking and non-blocking operations.

In order to manipulate the socket's blocking nature, we need to create a socket object first.

We can then call `setblocking(1)` to set up blocking or `setblocking(0)` to unset blocking. Finally, we bind the socket to a specific port and listen for incoming connections.

Listing 1.9 shows how the socket changes to blocking or non-blocking mode as follows:

```
#!/usr/bin/env python
# Python Network Programming Cookbook -- Chapter - 1
# This program is optimized for Python 2.7. It may run on any
# other Python version with/without modifications

import socket

def test_socket_modes():
    s = socket.socket(socket.AF_INET, socket.SOCK_STREAM)
    s.setblocking(1)
    s.settimeout(0.5)
    s.bind(("127.0.0.1", 0))

    socket_address = s.getsockname()
    print "Trivial Server launched on socket: %s" %str(socket_address)
    while(1):
        s.listen(1)

if __name__ == '__main__':
    test_socket_modes()
```

If you run this recipe, it will launch a trivial server that has the blocking mode enabled as shown in the following command:

```
$ python 1_9_socket_modes.py
Trivial Server launched on socket: ('127.0.0.1', 51410)
```

How it works...

In this recipe, we enable blocking on a socket by setting the value `1` in the `setblocking()` method. Similarly, you can unset the value `0` in this method to make it non-blocking.

This feature will be reused in some later recipes, where its real purpose will be elaborated.

Reusing socket addresses

You want to run a socket server always on a specific port even after it is closed intentionally or unexpectedly. This is useful in some cases where your client program always connects to that specific server port. So, you don't need to change the server port.

How to do it...

If you run a Python socket server on a specific port and try to rerun it after closing it once, you won't be able to use the same port. It will usually throw an error like the following command:

```
Traceback (most recent call last):
  File "1_10_reuse_socket_address.py", line 40, in <module>
    reuse_socket_addr()
  File "1_10_reuse_socket_address.py", line 25, in reuse_socket_addr
    srv.bind( ('', local_port) )
  File "<string>", line 1, in bind
socket.error: [Errno 98] Address already in use
```

The remedy to this problem is to enable the socket reuse option, `SO_REUSEADDR`.

After creating a socket object, we can query the state of address reuse, say an old state. Then, we call the `setsockopt()` method to alter the value of its address reuse state. Then, we follow the usual steps of binding to an address and listening for incoming client connections. In this example, we catch the `KeyboardInterrupt` exception so that if you issue *Ctrl* + *C*, then the Python script gets terminated without showing any exception message.

Listing 1.10 shows how to reuse socket addresses as follows:

```
#!/usr/bin/env python
# Python Network Programming Cookbook -- Chapter - 1
# This program is optimized for Python 2.7. It may run on any
# other Python version with/without modifications

import socket
import sys

def reuse_socket_addr():
    sock = socket.socket( socket.AF_INET, socket.SOCK_STREAM )

    # Get the old state of the SO_REUSEADDR option
    old_state = sock.getsockopt(socket.SOL_SOCKET, socket.SO_REUSEADDR
)
```

```
    print "Old sock state: %s" %old_state

    # Enable the SO_REUSEADDR option
    sock.setsockopt( socket.SOL_SOCKET, socket.SO_REUSEADDR, 1 )
    new_state = sock.getsockopt( socket.SOL_SOCKET, socket.SO_
REUSEADDR )
    print "New sock state: %s" %new_state

    local_port = 8282

    srv = socket.socket(socket.AF_INET, socket.SOCK_STREAM)
    srv.setsockopt(socket.SOL_SOCKET, socket.SO_REUSEADDR, 1)
    srv.bind( ('', local_port) )
    srv.listen(1)
    print ("Listening on port: %s " %local_port)
    while True:
        try:
            connection, addr = srv.accept()
            print 'Connected by %s:%s' % (addr[0], addr[1])
        except KeyboardInterrupt:
            break
        except socket.error, msg:
            print '%s' % (msg,)

if __name__ == '__main__':
    reuse_socket_e addr()
```

The output from this recipe will be similar to the following command:

```
$ python 1_10_reuse_socket_address.py
Old sock state: 0
New sock state: 1
Listening on port: 8282
```

How it works...

You may run this script from one console window and try to connect to this server from another console window by typing `telnet localhost 8282`. After you close the server program, you can rerun it again on the same port. However, if you comment out the line that sets the `SO_REUSEADDR`, the server will not run for the second time.

Printing the current time from the Internet time server

Many programs rely on the accurate machine time, such as the make command in UNIX. Your machine time may be different and need synchronizing with another time server in your network.

Getting ready

In order to synchronize your machine time with one of the Internet time servers, you can write a Python client for that. For this, ntplib will be used. Here, the client/server conversation will be done using **Network Time Protocol** (**NTP**). If ntplib is not installed on your machine, you can get it from PyPI with the following command using pip or easy_install:

```
$ pip install ntplib
```

How to do it...

We create an instance of NTPClient and then we call the request() method on it by passing the NTP server address.

Listing 1.11shows how to print the current time from the Internet time server is as follows:

```
#!/usr/bin/env python
# Python Network Programming Cookbook -- Chapter - 1
# This program is optimized for Python 2.7. It may run on any
# other Python version with/without modifications

import ntplib
from time import ctime

def print_time():
    ntp_client = ntplib.NTPClient()
    response = ntp_client.request('pool.ntp.org')
    print ctime(response.tx_time)

if __name__ == '__main__':
    print_time()
```

In my machine, this recipe shows the following output:

```
$ python 1_11_print_machine_time.py
Thu Mar 5 14:02:58 2012
```

How it works...

Here, an NTP client has been created and an NTP request has been sent to one of the Internet NTP servers, `pool.ntp.org`. The `ctime()` function is used for printing the response.

Writing a SNTP client

Unlike the previous recipe, sometimes, you don't need to get the precise time from the NTP server. You can use a simpler version of NTP called simple network time protocol.

How to do it...

Let us create a plain SNTP client without using any third-party library.

Let us first define two constants: `NTP_SERVER` and `TIME1970`. `NTP_SERVER` is the server address to which our client will connect, and `TIME1970` is the reference time on January 1, 1970 (also called *Epoch*). You may find the value of the Epoch time or convert to the Epoch time at `http://www.epochconverter.com/`. The actual client creates a UDP socket (`SOCK_DGRAM`) to connect to the server following the UDP protocol. The client then needs to send the SNTP protocol data (`'\x1b' + 47 * '\0'`) in a packet. Our UDP client sends and receives data using the `sendto()` and `recvfrom()` methods.

When the server returns the time information in a packed array, the client needs a specialized `struct` module to unpack the data. The only interesting data is located in the 11th element of the array. Finally, we need to subtract the reference value, `TIME1970`, from the unpacked value to get the actual current time.

Listing 1.11 shows how to write an SNTP client as follows:

```
#!/usr/bin/env python
# Python Network Programming Cookbook -- Chapter - 1
# This program is optimized for Python 2.7. It may run on any
# other Python version with/without modifications
import socket
import struct
import sys
import time

NTP_SERVER = "0.uk.pool.ntp.org"
TIME1970 = 2208988800L

def sntp_client():
    client = socket.socket(socket.AF_INET, socket.SOCK_DGRAM)
    data = '\x1b' + 47 * '\0'
```

```
        client.sendto(data, (NTP_SERVER, 123))
        data, address = client.recvfrom( 1024 )
        if data:
            print 'Response received from:', address
        t = struct.unpack( '!12I', data )[10]
        t -= TIME1970
        print '\tTime=%s' % time.ctime(t)

if __name__ == '__main__':
    sntp_client()
```

This recipe prints the current time from the Internet time server received with the SNTP protocol as follows:

```
$ python 1_12_sntp_client.py
Response received from: ('87.117.251.2', 123)
        Time=Tue Feb 25 14:49:38 2014
```

How it works...

This SNTP client creates a socket connection and sends the protocol data. After receiving the response from the NTP server (in this case, `0.uk.pool.ntp.org`), it unpacks the data with `struct`. Finally, it subtracts the reference time, which is January 1, 1970, and prints the time using the `ctime()` built-in method in the Python time module.

Writing a simple echo client/server application

After testing with basic socket APIs in Python, let us create a socket server and client now. Here, you will have the chance to utilize your basic knowledge gained in the previous recipes.

How to do it...

In this example, a server will echo whatever it receives from the client. We will use the Python `argparse` module to specify the TCP port from a command line. Both the server and client script will take this argument.

First, we create the server. We start by creating a TCP socket object. Then, we set the reuse address so that we can run the server as many times as we need. We bind the socket to the given port on our local machine. In the listening stage, we make sure we listen to multiple clients in a queue using the backlog argument to the `listen()` method. Finally, we wait for the client to be connected and send some data to the server. When the data is received, the server echoes back the data to the client.

Listing 1.13a shows how to write a simple echo client/server application as follows:

```
#!/usr/bin/env python
# Python Network Programming Cookbook -- Chapter - 1
# This program is optimized for Python 2.7. It may run on any
# other Python version with/without modifications.

import socket
import sys
import argparse

host = 'localhost'
data_payload = 2048
backlog = 5

def echo_server(port):
    """ A simple echo server """
    # Create a TCP socket
    sock = socket.socket(socket.AF_INET, socket.SOCK_STREAM)
    # Enable reuse address/port
    sock.setsockopt(socket.SOL_SOCKET, socket.SO_REUSEADDR, 1)
    # Bind the socket to the port
    server_address = (host, port)
    print "Starting up echo server  on %s port %s" % server_address
    sock.bind(server_address)
    # Listen to clients, backlog argument specifies the max no. of 
queued connections
    sock.listen(backlog)
    while True:
        print "Waiting to receive message from client"
        client, address = sock.accept()
        data = client.recv(data_payload)
        if data:
            print "Data: %s" %data
            client.send(data)
            print "sent %s bytes back to %s" % (data, address)
        # end connection
        client.close()

if __name__ == '__main__':
    parser = argparse.ArgumentParser(description='Socket Server 
Example')
    parser.add_argument('--port', action="store", dest="port", 
type=int, required=True)
    given_args = parser.parse_args()
    port = given_args.port
    echo_server(port)
```

On the client-side code, we create a client socket using the port argument and connect to the server. Then, the client sends the message, `Test message. This will be echoed` to the server, and the client immediately receives the message back in a few segments. Here, two try-except blocks are constructed to catch any exception during this interactive session.

Listing 1-13b shows the echo client as follows:

```
#!/usr/bin/env python
# Python Network Programming Cookbook -- Chapter - 1
# This program is optimized for Python 2.7. It may run on any
# other Python version with/without modifications.

import socket
import sys

import argparse

host = 'localhost'

def echo_client(port):
    """ A simple echo client """
    # Create a TCP/IP socket
    sock = socket.socket(socket.AF_INET, socket.SOCK_STREAM)
    # Connect the socket to the server
    server_address = (host, port)
    print "Connecting to %s port %s" % server_address
    sock.connect(server_address)

    # Send data
    try:
        # Send data
        message = "Test message. This will be echoed"
        print "Sending %s" % message
        sock.sendall(message)
        # Look for the response
        amount_received = 0
        amount_expected = len(message)
        while amount_received < amount_expected:
            data = sock.recv(16)
            amount_received += len(data)
            print "Received: %s" % data
    except socket.errno, e:
        print "Socket error: %s" %str(e)
    except Exception, e:
        print "Other exception: %s" %str(e)
    finally:
```

```
        print "Closing connection to the server"
        sock.close()

if __name__ == '__main__':
    parser = argparse.ArgumentParser(description='Socket Server 
Example')
    parser.add_argument('--port', action="store", dest="port", 
type=int, required=True)
    given_args = parser.parse_args()
    port = given_args.port
    echo_client(port)
```

How it works...

In order to see the client/server interactions, launch the following server script in one console:

```
$ python 1_13a_echo_server.py --port=9900
Starting up echo server  on localhost port 9900

Waiting to receive message from client
```

Now, run the client from another terminal as follows:

```
$ python 1_13b_echo_client.py --port=9900
Connecting to localhost port 9900
Sending Test message. This will be echoed
Received: Test message. Th
Received: is will be echoe
Received: d
Closing connection to the server
```

Upon connecting to the localhost, the client server will also print the following message:

```
Data: Test message. This will be echoed
sent Test message. This will be echoed bytes back to ('127.0.0.1', 42961)
Waiting to receive message from client
```

2

Multiplexing Socket I/O for Better Performance

In this chapter, we will cover the following recipes:

- Using ForkingMixIn in your socket server applications
- Using ThreadingMixIn in your socket server applications
- Writing a chat server using select.select
- Multiplexing a web server using select.epoll
- Multiplexing an echo server using Diesel concurrent library

Introduction

This chapter focuses on improving the socket server performance using a few useful techniques. Unlike the previous chapter, here we consider multiple clients that will be connected to the server and the communication can be asynchronous. The server does not need to process the request from clients in a blocking manner, this can be done independent of each other. If one client takes more time to receive or process data, the server does not need to wait for that. It can talk to other clients using separate threads or processes.

In this chapter, we will also explore the `select` module that provides the platform-specific I/O monitoring functions. This module is built on top of the select system call of the underlying operating system's kernel. For Linux, the manual page is located at `http://man7.org/linux/man-pages/man2/select.2.html` and can be checked to see the available features of this system call. Since our socket server would like to interact with many clients, `select` can be very helpful to monitor non-blocking sockets. There are some third-party Python libraries that can also help us to deal with multiple clients at the same time. We have included one sample recipe of using Diesel concurrent library.

Although, for the sake of brevity, we will be using two or few clients, readers are free to extend the recipes of this chapter and use them with tens and hundreds of clients.

Using ForkingMixIn in your socket server applications

You have decided to write an asynchronous Python socket server application. The server will not block in processing a client request. So the server needs a mechanism to deal with each client independently.

Python 2.7 version's `SocketServer` class comes with two utility classes: `ForkingMixIn` and `ThreadingMixIn`. The `ForkingMixin` class will spawn a new process for each client request. This class is discussed in this section. The `ThreadingMixIn` class will be discussed in the next section. For more information, you can refer to the Python documentation at `http://docs.python.org/2/library/socketserver.html`.

How to do it...

Let us rewrite our echo server, previously described in *Chapter 1, Sockets, IPv4, and Simple Client/Server Programming*. We can utilize the subclasses of the `SocketServer` class family. It has ready-made TCP, UDP, and other protocol servers. We can create a `ForkingServer` class inherited from `TCPServer` and `ForkingMixin`. The former parent will enable our `ForkingServer` class to do all the necessary server operations that we did manually before, such as creating a socket, binding to an address, and listening for incoming connections. Our server also needs to inherit from `ForkingMixin` to handle clients asynchronously.

The `ForkingServer` class also needs to set up a request handler that dictates how to handle a client request. Here our server will echo back the text string received from the client. Our request handler class `ForkingServerRequestHandler` is inherited from the `BaseRequestHandler` provided with the `SocketServer` library.

We can code the client of our echo server, `ForkingClient`, in an object-oriented fashion. In Python, the constructor method of a class is called `__init__()`. By convention, it takes a self-argument to attach attributes or properties of that particular class. The `ForkingClient` echo server will be initialized at `__init__()` and sends the message to the server at the `run()` method respectively.

If you are not familiar with **object-oriented programming** (**OOP**) at all, it might be helpful to review the basic concepts of OOP while attempting to grasp this recipe.

In order to test our `ForkingServer` class, we can launch multiple echo clients and see how the server responds back to the clients.

Listing 2.1 shows a sample code using `ForkingMixin` in a socket server application as follows:

```
#!/usr/bin/env python
# Python Network Programming Cookbook -- Chapter - 2
# This program is optimized for Python 2.7.
# It may run on any other version with/without modifications.
# See more: http://docs.python.org/2/library/socketserver.html

import os
import socket
import threading
import SocketServer


SERVER_HOST = 'localhost'
SERVER_PORT = 0 # tells the kernel to pick up a port dynamically
BUF_SIZE = 1024
ECHO_MSG = 'Hello echo server!'


class ForkedClient():
    """ A client to test forking server"""
    def __init__(self, ip, port):
        # Create a socket
        self.sock = socket.socket(socket.AF_INET, socket.SOCK_STREAM)
        # Connect to the server
        self.sock.connect((ip, port))

    def run(self):
        """ Client playing with the server"""
        # Send the data to server
        current_process_id = os.getpid()
        print 'PID %s Sending echo message to the server : "%s"' %
(current_process_id, ECHO_MSG)
        sent_data_length = self.sock.send(ECHO_MSG)
        print "Sent: %d characters, so far..." %sent_data_length

        # Display server response
        response = self.sock.recv(BUF_SIZE)
        print "PID %s received: %s" % (current_process_id,
response[5:])

    def shutdown(self):
        """ Cleanup the client socket """
        self.sock.close()


class ForkingServerRequestHandler(SocketServer.BaseRequestHandler):
```

```
    def handle(self):
        # Send the echo back to the client
        data = self.request.recv(BUF_SIZE)
        current_process_id = os.getpid()
        response = '%s: %s' % (current_process_id, data)
        print "Server sending response [current_process_id: data] =
[%s]" %response
        self.request.send(response)
        return


class ForkingServer(SocketServer.ForkingMixIn,
                    SocketServer.TCPServer,
                    ):
    """Nothing to add here, inherited everything necessary from
parents"""
    pass


def main():
    # Launch the server
    server = ForkingServer((SERVER_HOST, SERVER_PORT),
ForkingServerRequestHandler)
    ip, port = server.server_address # Retrieve the port number
    server_thread = threading.Thread(target=server.serve_forever)
    server_thread.setDaemon(True) # don't hang on exit
    server_thread.start()
    print 'Server loop running PID: %s' %os.getpid()

    # Launch the client(s)
    client1 =  ForkedClient(ip, port)
    client1.run()

    client2 =  ForkedClient(ip, port)
    client2.run()

    # Clean them up
    server.shutdown()
    client1.shutdown()
    client2.shutdown()
    server.socket.close()

if __name__ == '__main__':
    main()
```

How it works...

An instance of `ForkingServer` is launched in the main thread, which has been daemonized to run in the background. Now, the two clients have started interacting with the server.

If you run the script, it will show the following output:

```
$ python 2_1_forking_mixin_socket_server.py
Server loop running PID: 12608
PID 12608 Sending echo message to the server : "Hello echo server!"
Sent: 18 characters, so far...
Server sending response [current_process_id: data] = [12610: Hello echo server!]
PID 12608 received: : Hello echo server!
PID 12608 Sending echo message to the server : "Hello echo server!"
Sent: 18 characters, so far...
Server sending response [current_process_id: data] = [12611: Hello echo server!]
PID 12608 received: : Hello echo server!
```

The server port number might be different in your machine since this is dynamically chosen by the operating system kernel.

Using ThreadingMixIn in your socket server applications

Perhaps you prefer writing a multi-threaded application over a process-based one due to any particular reason, for example, sharing the states of that application across threads, avoiding the complexity of inter-process communication, or something else. In such a situation, if you like to write an asynchronous network server using `SocketServer` library, you will need `ThreadingMixin`.

Getting ready

By making a few minor changes to our previous recipe, you can get a working version of socket server using `ThreadingMixin`.

> **Downloading the example code**
>
> You can download the example code files for all Packt books you have purchased from your account at `http://www.packtpub.com`. If you purchased this book elsewhere, you can visit `http://www.packtpub.com/support` and register to have the files e-mailed directly to you.

How to do it...

As seen in the previous socket server based on `ForkingMixIn`, `ThreadingMixIn` socket server will follow the same coding pattern of an echo server except a few things. First, our `ThreadedTCPServer` will inherit from `TCPServer` and `TheadingMixIn`. This multi-threaded version will launch a new thread when a client connects to it. Some more details can be found at `http://docs.python.org/2/library/socketserver.html`.

The request handler class of our socket server, `ForkingServerRequestHandler`, sends the echo back to the client from a new thread. You can check the thread information here. For the sake of simplicity, we put the client code in a function instead of a class. The client code creates the client socket and sends the message to the server.

Listing 2.2 shows a sample code on echo socket server using `ThreadingMixIn` as follows:

```
#!/usr/bin/env python
# Python Network Programming Cookbook -- Chapter - 2
# This program is optimized for Python 2.7
# It may run on any other version with/without modifications.
import os
import socket
import threading
import SocketServer
SERVER_HOST = 'localhost'
SERVER_PORT = 0 # tells the kernel to pick up a port dynamically
BUF_SIZE = 1024

def client(ip, port, message):
    """ A client to test threading mixin server"""
    # Connect to the server
    sock = socket.socket(socket.AF_INET, socket.SOCK_STREAM)
    sock.connect((ip, port))
    try:
        sock.sendall(message)
        response = sock.recv(BUF_SIZE)
        print "Client received: %s" %response
    finally:
        sock.close()

class ThreadedTCPRequestHandler(SocketServer.BaseRequestHandler):
    """ An example of threaded TCP request handler """
    def handle(self):
        data = self.request.recv(1024)
        current_thread = threading.current_thread()
        response = "%s: %s" %(current_thread.name, data)
        self.request.sendall(response)
```

```
class ThreadedTCPServer(SocketServer.ThreadingMixIn, SocketServer.
TCPServer):
    """Nothing to add here, inherited everything necessary from
parents"""
    pass
if __name__ == "__main__":
    # Run server
    server = ThreadedTCPServer((SERVER_HOST, SERVER_PORT),
ThreadedTCPRequestHandler)
    ip, port = server.server_address # retrieve ip address
    # Start a thread with the server -- one  thread per request
    server_thread = threading.Thread(target=server.serve_forever)
    # Exit the server thread when the main thread exits
    server_thread.daemon = True
    server_thread.start()
    print "Server loop running on thread: %s"  %server_thread.name
    # Run clients
    client(ip, port, "Hello from client 1")
    client(ip, port, "Hello from client 2")
    client(ip, port, "Hello from client 3")
    # Server cleanup
    server.shutdown()
```

How it works...

This recipe first creates a server thread and launches it in the background. Then it launches three test clients to send messages to the server. In response, the server echoes back the message to the clients. In the `handle()` method of the server's request handler, you can see that we retrieve the current thread information and print it. This should be different in each client connection.

In this client/server conversation, the `sendall()` method has been used to guarantee the sending of all data without any loss:

```
$ python 2_2_threading_mixin_socket_server.py
Server loop running on thread: Thread-1
Client received: Thread-2: Hello from client 1
Client received: Thread-3: Hello from client 2
Client received: Thread-4: Hello from client 3
```

Writing a chat server using select.select

Launching a separate thread or process per client may not be viable in any larger network server application where several hundred or thousand clients are concurrently connected to the server. Due to the limited available memory and host CPU power, we need a better technique to deal with large number of clients. Fortunately, Python provides the `select` module to overcome this problem.

How to do it...

We need to write an efficient chat server that can handle several hundred or a large number of client connections. We will use the `select()` method from the `select` module that will enable our chat server and client to do any task without blocking a send or receive call all the time.

Let us design this recipe such that a single script can launch both client and server with an additional `--name` argument. Only if `--name=server` is passed from the command line, the script will launch the chat server. Any other value passed to the `--name` argument, for example, `client1`, `client2`, will launch a chat client. Let's specify our char server port number from the command line using `--port` argument. For a larger application, it may be preferable to write separate modules for the server and client.

Listing 2.3 shows an example of chat application using `select.select` as follows:

```
#!/usr/bin/env python
# Python Network Programming Cookbook -- Chapter - 2
# This program is optimized for Python 2.7
# It may run on any other version with/without modifications
import select
import socket
import sys
import signal
import cPickle
import struct
import argparse

SERVER_HOST = 'localhost'
CHAT_SERVER_NAME = 'server'

# Some utilities
def send(channel, *args):
    buffer = cPickle.dumps(args)
    value = socket.htonl(len(buffer))
    size = struct.pack("L",value)
```

```
        channel.send(size)
        channel.send(buffer)

    def receive(channel):
        size = struct.calcsize("L")
        size = channel.recv(size)
        try:
            size = socket.ntohl(struct.unpack("L", size)[0])
        except struct.error, e:
            return ''
        buf = ""
        while len(buf) < size:
            buf = channel.recv(size - len(buf))
        return cPickle.loads(buf)[0]
```

The `send()` method takes one named argument channel and positional argument `*args`. It serializes the data using the `dumps()` method from the `cPickle` module. It determines the size of the data using the `struct` module. Similarly, `receive()` takes one named argument `channel`.

Now we can code the `ChatServer` class as follows:

```
    class ChatServer(object):
        """ An example chat server using select """
     def __init__(self, port, backlog=5):
       self.clients = 0
       self.clientmap = {}
       self.outputs = [] # list output sockets
       self.server = socket.socket(socket.AF_INET, socket.SOCK_STREAM)
       # Enable re-using socket address
       self.server.setsockopt(socket.SOL_SOCKET, socket.SO_REUSEADDR, 1)
       self.server.bind((SERVER_HOST, port))
       print 'Server listening to port: %s ...' %port
       self.server.listen(backlog)
       # Catch keyboard interrupts
       signal.signal(signal.SIGINT, self.sighandler)

        def sighandler(self, signum, frame):
            """ Clean up client outputs"""
            # Close the server
            print 'Shutting down server...'
            # Close existing client sockets
            for output in self.outputs:
                output.close()
            self.server.close()
```

```
    def get_client_name(self, client):
        """ Return the name of the client """
        info = self.clientmap[client]
        host, name = info[0][0], info[1]
        return '@'.join((name, host))
```

Now the main executable method of the `ChatServer` class should look like the following code:

```
    def run(self):
        inputs = [self.server, sys.stdin]
        self.outputs = []
        running = True
        while running:
         try:
          readable, writeable, exceptional = \
          select.select(inputs, self.outputs, [])
            except select.error, e:
                break
            for sock in readable:
                if sock == self.server:
                    # handle the server socket
                    client, address = self.server.accept()
                    print "Chat server: got connection %d from %s" %\
(client.fileno(), address)
                    # Read the login name
                    cname = receive(client).split('NAME: ')[1]
                    # Compute client name and send back
                    self.clients += 1
                    send(client, 'CLIENT: ' + str(address[0]))
                    inputs.append(client)
                    self.clientmap[client] = (address, cname)
                    # Send joining information to other clients
                    msg = "\n(Connected: New client (%d) from %s)" %\
(self.clients, self.get_client_name(client))
                    for output in self.outputs:
                        send(output, msg)
                    self.outputs.append(client)
                elif sock == sys.stdin:
                    # handle standard input
                    junk = sys.stdin.readline()
                    running = False
                else:
                    # handle all other sockets
                    try:
                        data = receive(sock)
                        if data:
                            # Send as new client's message...
```

```
                    msg = '\n#[' + self.get_client_name(sock)\
                           + ']>>' + data
                    # Send data to all except ourself
                    for output in self.outputs:
                        if output != sock:
                            send(output, msg)
                else:
                    print "Chat server: %d hung up" % \
                    sock.fileno()
                    self.clients -= 1
                    sock.close()
                    inputs.remove(sock)
                    self.outputs.remove(sock)
                    # Sending client leaving info to others
                    msg = "\n(Now hung up: Client from %s)" %\
    self.get_client_name(sock)
                    for output in self.outputs:
                        send(output, msg)
            except socket.error, e:
                # Remove
                inputs.remove(sock)
                self.outputs.remove(sock)
        self.server.close()
```

The chat server initializes with a few data attributes. It stores the count of clients, map of each client, and output sockets. The usual server socket creation also sets the option to reuse an address so that there is no problem restarting the server again using the same port. An optional backlog argument to the chat server constructor sets the maximum number of queued connections to listen by the server.

An interesting aspect of this chat server is to catch the user interrupt, usually via keyboard, using the `signal` module. So a signal handler `sighandler` is registered for the interrupt signal (`SIGINT`). This signal handler catches the keyboard interrupt signal and closes all output sockets where data may be waiting to be sent.

The main executive method of our chat server `run()` performs its operation inside a `while` loop. This method registers with a select interface where the input argument is the chat server socket, `stdin`. The output argument is specified by the server's output socket list. In return, `select` provides three lists: readable, writable, and exceptional sockets. The chat server is only interested in readable sockets where some data is ready to be read. If that socket indicates to itself, then that will mean a new client connection has been established. So the server retrieves the client's name and broadcasts this information to other clients. In another case, if anything comes from the input arguments, the chat server exits. Similarly, the chat server deals with the other client's socket inputs. It relays the data received from any client to others and also shares their joining/leaving information.

The chat client code class should contain the following code:

```
class ChatClient(object):
    """ A command line chat client using select """

    def __init__(self, name, port, host=SERVER_HOST):
        self.name = name
        self.connected = False
        self.host = host
        self.port = port
        # Initial prompt
        self.prompt='[' + '@'.join((name, socket.gethostname().
split('.')[0])) + ']> '
        # Connect to server at port
        try:
            self.sock = socket.socket(socket.AF_INET, socket.SOCK_
STREAM)
            self.sock.connect((host, self.port))
            print "Now connected to chat server@ port %d" % self.port
            self.connected = True
            # Send my name...
            send(self.sock,'NAME: ' + self.name)
            data = receive(self.sock)
            # Contains client address, set it
            addr = data.split('CLIENT: ')[1]
            self.prompt = '[' + '@'.join((self.name, addr)) + ']> '
        except socket.error, e:
            print "Failed to connect to chat server @ port %d" % self.
port
            sys.exit(1)

    def run(self):
        """ Chat client main loop """
        while self.connected:
            try:
                sys.stdout.write(self.prompt)
                sys.stdout.flush()
                # Wait for input from stdin and socket
                readable, writeable,exceptional = select.select([0,
self.sock], [],[])
                for sock in readable:
                    if sock == 0:
                        data = sys.stdin.readline().strip()
                        if data: send(self.sock, data)
                    elif sock == self.sock:
```

```
                        data = receive(self.sock)
                        if not data:
                            print 'Client shutting down.'
                            self.connected = False
                            break
                        else:
                            sys.stdout.write(data + '\n')
                            sys.stdout.flush()

            except KeyboardInterrupt:
                print " Client interrupted. """
                self.sock.close()
                break
```

The chat client initializes with a name argument and sends this name to the chat server upon connecting. It also sets up a custom prompt `[ name@host ]>`. The executive method of this client `run()` continues its operation as long as the connection to the server is active. In a manner similar to the chat server, the chat client also registers with `select()`. If anything in readable sockets is ready, it enables the client to receive data. If the sock value is `0` and there's any data available then the data can be sent. The same information is also shown in stdout or, in our case, the command-line console. Our main method should now get command-line arguments and call either the server or client as follows:

```
if __name__ == "__main__":
    parser = argparse.ArgumentParser(description='Socket Server 
Example with Select')
    parser.add_argument('--name', action="store", dest="name", 
required=True)
    parser.add_argument('--port', action="store", dest="port", 
type=int, required=True)
    given_args = parser.parse_args()
    port = given_args.port
    name = given_args.name
    if name == CHAT_SERVER_NAME:
        server = ChatServer(port)
        server.run()
    else:
        client = ChatClient(name=name, port=port)
        client.run()
```

We would like to run this script thrice: once for the chat server and twice for two chat clients. For the server, we pass `-name=server` and `port=8800`. For `client1`, we change the name argument `--name=client1` and for `client2`, we put `--name=client2`. Then from the `client1` value prompt we send the message `"Hello from client 1"`, which is printed in the prompt of the `client2`. Similarly, we send `"hello from client 2"` from the prompt of the `client2`, which is shown in the prompt of the `client1`.

The output for the server is as follows:

```
$ python 2_3_chat_server_with_select.py --name=server --port=8800
Server listening to port: 8800 ...
Chat server: got connection 4 from ('127.0.0.1', 56565)
Chat server: got connection 5 from ('127.0.0.1', 56566)
```

The output for `client1` is as follows:

```
$ python 2_3_chat_server_with_select.py --name=client1 --port=8800
Now connected to chat server@ port 8800
[client1@127.0.0.1]>
(Connected: New client (2) from client2@127.0.0.1)
[client1@127.0.0.1]> Hello from client 1
[client1@127.0.0.1]>
#[client2@127.0.0.1]>>hello from client 2
```

The output for `client2` is as follows:

```
$ python 2_3_chat_server_with_select.py --name=client2 --port=8800
Now connected to chat server@ port 8800
[client2@127.0.0.1]>
#[client1@127.0.0.1]>>Hello from client 1
[client2@127.0.0.1]> hello from client 2
[client2@127.0.0.1]
```

The whole interaction is shown in the following screenshot:

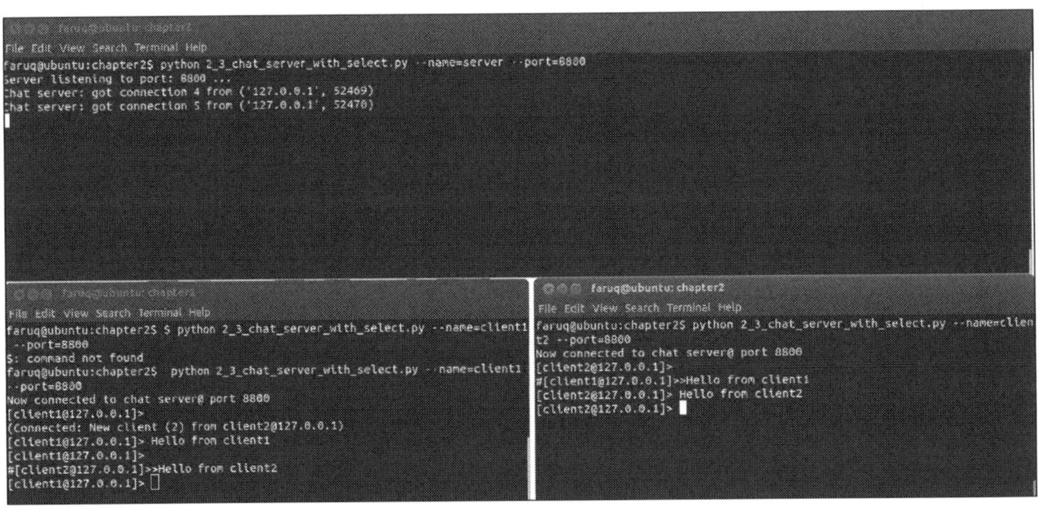

How it works...

At the top of our module, we defined two utility functions: `send()` and `receive()`.

The chat server and client use these utility functions, which were demonstrated earlier. The details of the chat server and client methods were also discussed earlier.

Multiplexing a web server using select.epoll

Python's `select` module has a few platform-specific, networking event management functions. On a Linux machine, `epoll` is available. This will utilize the operating system kernel that will poll network events and let our script know whenever something happens. This sounds more efficient than the previously mentioned `select.select` approach.

How to do it...

Let's write a simple web server that can return a single line of text to any connected web browser.

The core idea is during the initialization of this web server, we should make a call to `select.epoll()` and register our server's file descriptor for event notifications. In the web server's executive code, the socket event is monitored as follows:

```
Listing 2.4 Simple web server using select.epoll
#!/usr/bin/env python
# Python Network Programming Cookbook -- Chapter - 2
# This program is optimized for Python 2.7
# It may run on any other version with/without modifications.
import socket
import select
import argparse
SERVER_HOST = 'localhost'
EOL1 = b'\n\n'
EOL2 = b'\n\r\n'
SERVER_RESPONSE  = b"""HTTP/1.1 200 OK\r\nDate: Mon, 1 Apr 2013
01:01:01 GMT\r\nContent-Type: text/plain\r\nContent-Length: 25\r\n\r\n
Hello from Epoll Server!"""

class EpollServer(object):
    """ A socket server using Epoll"""
    def __init__(self, host=SERVER_HOST, port=0):
      self.sock = socket.socket(socket.AF_INET, socket.SOCK_STREAM)
      self.sock.setsockopt(socket.SOL_SOCKET, socket.SO_REUSEADDR, 1)
      self.sock.bind((host, port))
      self.sock.listen(1)
      self.sock.setblocking(0)
      self.sock.setsockopt(socket.IPPROTO_TCP, socket.TCP_NODELAY, 1)
```

```
        print "Started Epoll Server"
        self.epoll = select.epoll()
        self.epoll.register(self.sock.fileno(), select.EPOLLIN)

    def run(self):
     """Executes epoll server operation"""
     try:
        connections = {}; requests = {}; responses = {}
        while True:
      events = self.epoll.poll(1)
      for fileno, event in events:
        if fileno == self.sock.fileno():
          connection, address = self.sock.accept()
          connection.setblocking(0)
          self.epoll.register(connection.fileno(), select.EPOLLIN)
          connections[connection.fileno()] = connection
          requests[connection.fileno()] = b''
          responses[connection.fileno()] = SERVER_RESPONSE
        elif event & select.EPOLLIN:
          requests[fileno] += connections[fileno].recv(1024)
          if EOL1 in requests[fileno] or EOL2 in requests[fileno]:
                self.epoll.modify(fileno, select.EPOLLOUT)
                print('-'*40 + '\n' + requests[fileno].decode()[:-2])
         elif event & select.EPOLLOUT:
            byteswritten = connections[fileno].send(responses[fileno])
            responses[fileno] = responses[fileno][byteswritten:]
            if len(responses[fileno]) == 0:
                self.epoll.modify(fileno, 0)
                connections[fileno].shutdown(socket.SHUT_RDWR)
            elif event & select.EPOLLHUP:
                 self.epoll.unregister(fileno)
                 connections[fileno].close()
                 del connections[fileno]
     finally:
       self.epoll.unregister(self.sock.fileno())
       self.epoll.close()
       self.sock.close()

    if __name__ == '__main__':
     parser = argparse.ArgumentParser(description='Socket Server Example
    with Epoll')
     parser.add_argument('--port', action="store", dest="port", type=int,
    required=True)
        given_args = parser.parse_args()
        port = given_args.port
        server = EpollServer(host=SERVER_HOST, port=port)
        server.run()
```

If you run this script and access the web server from your browser, such as Firefox or IE, by entering `http://localhost:8800/`, the following output will be shown in the console:

```
$ python 2_4_simple_web_server_with_epoll.py --port=8800
Started Epoll Server
----------------------------------------
GET / HTTP/1.1
Host: localhost:8800
Connection: keep-alive
Accept: text/html,application/xhtml+xml,application/xml;q=0.9,*/*;q=0.8
User-Agent: Mozilla/5.0 (X11; Linux i686) AppleWebKit/537.31 (KHTML, like Gecko) Chrome/26.0.1410.43 Safari/537.31
DNT: 1
Accept-Encoding: gzip,deflate,sdch
Accept-Language: en-GB,en-US;q=0.8,en;q=0.6
Accept-Charset: ISO-8859-1,utf-8;q=0.7,*;q=0.3
Cookie: MoodleSession=69149dqnvhett7br3qebsrcmh1; MOODLEID1_=%257F%25BA%2B%2540V


----------------------------------------
GET /favicon.ico HTTP/1.1
Host: localhost:8800
Connection: keep-alive
Accept: */*
DNT: 1
User-Agent: Mozilla/5.0 (X11; Linux i686) AppleWebKit/537.31 (KHTML, like Gecko) Chrome/26.0.1410.43 Safari/537.31
Accept-Encoding: gzip,deflate,sdch
Accept-Language: en-GB,en-US;q=0.8,en;q=0.6
Accept-Charset: ISO-8859-1,utf-8;q=0.7,*;q=0.3
```

You will also be able to see the following line in your browser:

```
Hello from Epoll Server!
```

The following screenshot shows the scenario:

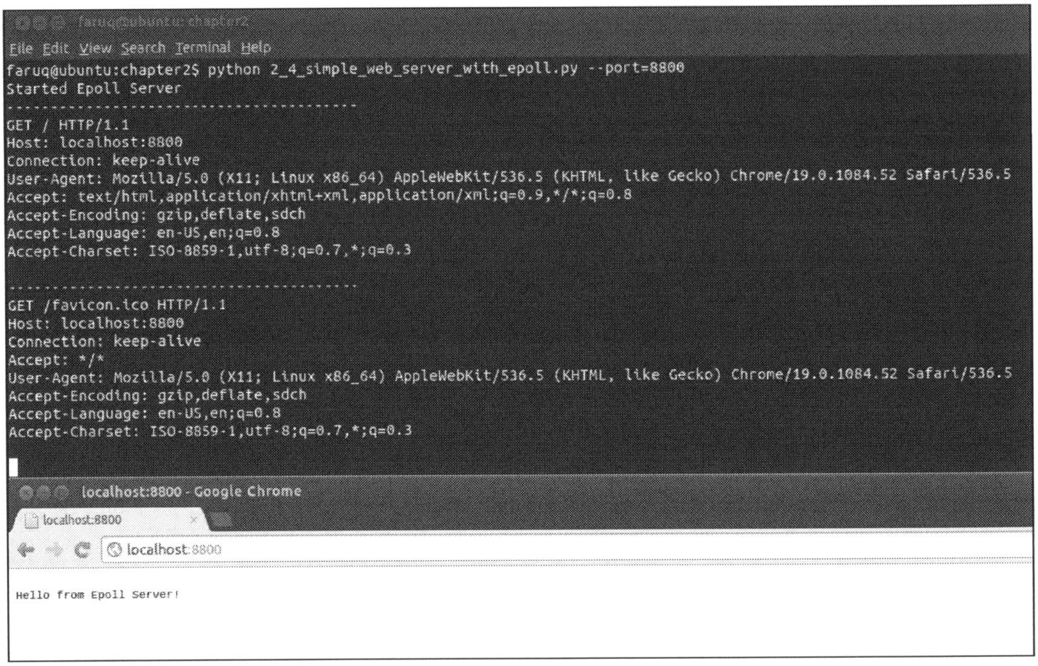

How it works...

In our `EpollServer` web server's constructor, a socket server is created and bound to a localhost at a given port. The server's socket is set to the non-blocking mode (`setblocking(0)`). The `TCP_NODELAY` option is also set so that our server can exchange data without buffering (as in the case of an SSH connection). Next, the `select.epoll()` instance is created and the socket's file descriptor is passed to that instance to help monitoring.

In the `run()` method of the web server, it starts receiving the socket events. These events are denoted as follows:

- `EPOLLIN`: This socket reads events
- `EPOLLOUT`: This socket writes events

In case of a server socket, it sets up the response `SERVER_RESPONSE`. When the socket has any connection that wants to write data, it can do that inside the `EPOLLOUT` event case. The `EPOLLHUP` event signals an unexpected close to a socket that is due to the internal error conditions.

Multiplexing an echo server using Diesel concurrent library

Sometimes you need to write a large custom networking application that wants to avoid repeated server initialization code that creates a socket, binds to an address, listens, and handles basic errors. There are numerous Python networking libraries out there to help you to remove boiler-plate code. Here, we can examine such a library called Diesel.

Getting ready

Diesel uses a non-blocking technique with co-routines to write networking severs efficiently. As stated on the website, *Diesel's core is a tight event loop that uses epoll to deliver nearly flat performance out to 10,000 connections and beyond*. Here, we introduce Diesel with a simple echo server. You also need diesel library 3.0 or any later version. You can do that with pip command: `$ pip install diesel >= 3.0`.

How to do it...

In the Python Diesel framework, applications are initialized with an instance of the `Application()` class and an event handler is registered with this instance. Let's see how simple it is to write an echo server.

Listing 2.5 shows the code on the echo server example using Diesel as follows:

```
#!/usr/bin/env python
# Python Network Programming Cookbook -- Chapter - 2
# This program is optimized for Python 2.7.
# It may run on any other version with/without modifications.
# You also need diesel library 3.0 or any later version

import diesel
import argparse

class EchoServer(object):
    """ An echo server using diesel"""

    def handler(self, remote_addr):
        """Runs the echo server"""
        host, port = remote_addr[0], remote_addr[1]
        print "Echo client connected from: %s:%d" %(host, port)

        while True:
            try:
```

```
                message = diesel.until_eol()
                your_message = ': '.join(['You said', message])
                diesel.send(your_message)
            except Exception, e:
                print "Exception:",e

def main(server_port):
    app = diesel.Application()
    server = EchoServer()
    app.add_service(diesel.Service(server.handler, server_port))
    app.run()

if __name__ == '__main__':
    parser = argparse.ArgumentParser(description='Echo server example
with Diesel')
    parser.add_argument('--port', action="store", dest="port",
type=int, required=True)
    given_args = parser.parse_args()
    port = given_args.port
    main(port)
```

If you run this script, the server will show the following output:

```
$ python 2_5_echo_server_with_diesel.py --port=8800
[2013/04/08 11:48:32] {diesel} WARNING:Starting diesel <hand-rolled
select.epoll>
Echo client connected from: 127.0.0.1:56603
```

On another console window, another Telnet client can be launched and the echoing message to our server can be tested as follows:

```
$ telnet localhost 8800
Trying 127.0.0.1...
Connected to localhost.
Escape character is '^]'.
Hello Diesel server ?
You said: Hello Diesel server ?
```

The following screenshot illustrates the interaction of the Diesel chat server:

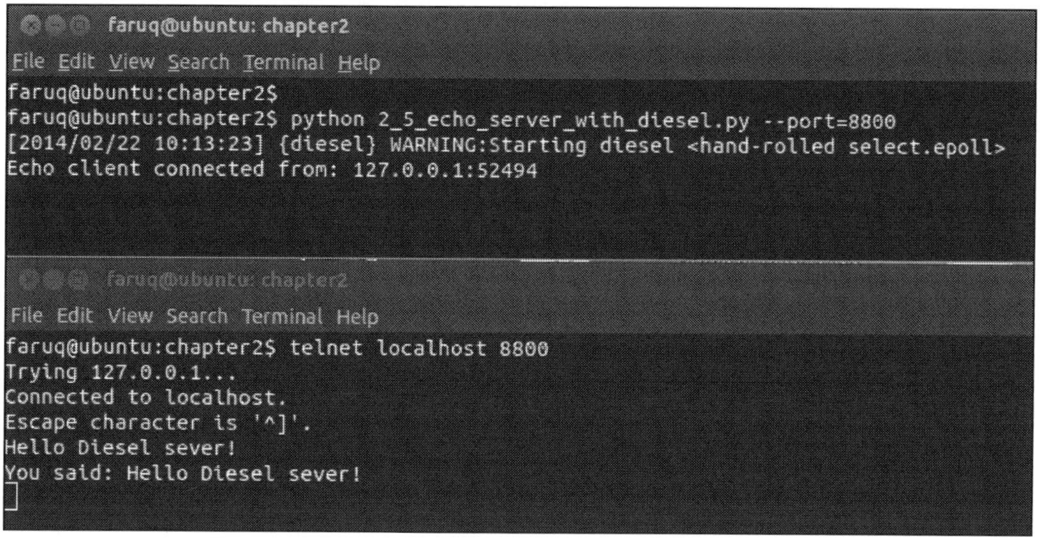

How it works...

Our script has taken a command-line argument for `--port` and passed this to the `main()` function where our Diesel application has been initialized and run.

Diesel has a notion of service where an application can be built with many services. `EchoServer` has a `handler()` method. This enables the server to deal with individual client connections. The `Service()` method takes the `handler` method and a port number to run that service.

Inside the `handler()` method, we determine the behavior of the server. In this case, the server is simply returning the message text.

If we compare this code with *Chapter 1, Sockets, IPv4, and Simple Client/Server Programming*, in the *Writing a simple echo client/server application* recipe (*listing 1.13a*), it is very clear that we do not need to write any boiler-plate code and hence it's very easy to concentrate on high-level application logic.

3
IPv6, Unix Domain Sockets, and Network Interfaces

In this chapter, we will cover the following topics:

- Forwarding a local port to a remote host
- Pinging hosts on the network with ICMP
- Waiting for a remote network service
- Enumerating interfaces on your machine
- Finding the IP address for a specific interface on your machine
- Finding whether an interface is up on your machine
- Detecting inactive machines on your network
- Performing a basic IPC using connected sockets (socketpair)
- Performing IPC using Unix domain sockets
- Finding out if your Python supports IPv6 sockets
- Extracting an IPv6 prefix from an IPv6 address
- Writing an IPv6 echo client/server

Introduction

This chapter extends the use of Python's socket library with a few third-party libraries. It also discusses some advanced techniques, for example, the asynchronous `ayncore` module from the Python standard library. This chapter also touches upon various protocols, ranging from an ICMP ping to an IPv6 client/server.

In this chapter, a few useful Python third-party modules have been introduced by some example recipes. For example, the network packet capture library, **Scapy**, is well known among Python network programmers.

A few recipes have been dedicated to explore the IPv6 utilities in Python including an IPv6 client/server. Some other recipes cover Unix domain sockets.

Forwarding a local port to a remote host

Sometimes, you may need to create a local port forwarder that will redirect all traffic from a local port to a particular remote host. This might be useful to enable proxy users to browse a certain site while preventing them from browsing some others.

How to do it...

Let us create a local port forwarding script that will redirect all traffic received at port 8800 to the Google home page (`http://www.google.com`). We can pass the local and remote host as well as port number to this script. For the sake of simplicity, let's only specify the local port number as we are aware that the web server runs on port 80.

Listing 3.1 shows a port forwarding example, as follows:

```
#!/usr/bin/env python
# Python Network Programming Cookbook -- Chapter - 3
# This program is optimized for Python 2.7.
# It may run on any other version with/without modifications.

import argparse
LOCAL_SERVER_HOST = 'localhost'
REMOTE_SERVER_HOST = 'www.google.com'
BUFSIZE = 4096
import asyncore
import socket
```

First, we define the `PortForwarder` class:

```
class PortForwarder(asyncore.dispatcher):
    def __init__(self, ip, port, remoteip,remoteport,backlog=5):
        asyncore.dispatcher.__init__(self)
        self.remoteip=remoteip
        self.remoteport=remoteport
        self.create_socket(socket.AF_INET,socket.SOCK_STREAM)
        self.set_reuse_addr()
        self.bind((ip,port))
        self.listen(backlog)
    def handle_accept(self):
        conn, addr = self.accept()
        print "Connected to:",addr
        Sender(Receiver(conn),self.remoteip,self.remoteport)
```

Now, we need to specify the `Receiver` and `Sender` classes, as follows:

```
class Receiver(asyncore.dispatcher):
    def __init__(self,conn):
        asyncore.dispatcher.__init__(self,conn)
        self.from_remote_buffer=''
        self.to_remote_buffer=''
        self.sender=None
    def handle_connect(self):
        pass
    def handle_read(self):
        read = self.recv(BUFSIZE)
        self.from_remote_buffer += read
    def writable(self):
        return (len(self.to_remote_buffer) > 0)
    def handle_write(self):
        sent = self.send(self.to_remote_buffer)
        self.to_remote_buffer = self.to_remote_buffer[sent:]
    def handle_close(self):
        self.close()
        if self.sender:
            self.sender.close()
class Sender(asyncore.dispatcher):
    def __init__(self, receiver, remoteaddr,remoteport):
        asyncore.dispatcher.__init__(self)
        self.receiver=receiver
        receiver.sender=self
        self.create_socket(socket.AF_INET, socket.SOCK_STREAM)
        self.connect((remoteaddr, remoteport))
```

```
    def handle_connect(self):
        pass
    def handle_read(self):
        read = self.recv(BUFSIZE)
        self.receiver.to_remote_buffer += read
    def writable(self):
        return (len(self.receiver.from_remote_buffer) > 0)
    def handle_write(self):
        sent = self.send(self.receiver.from_remote_buffer)
        self.receiver.from_remote_buffer = self.receiver.from_remote_
buffer[sent:]
    def handle_close(self):
        self.close()
        self.receiver.close()

if __name__ == "__main__":
    parser = argparse.ArgumentParser(description='Port forwarding
example')
    parser.add_argument('--local-host', action="store", dest="local_
host", default=LOCAL_SERVER_HOST)
    parser.add_argument('--local-port', action="store", dest="local_
port", type=int, required=True)
    parser.add_argument('--remote-host', action="store", dest="remote_
host",  default=REMOTE_SERVER_HOST)
    parser.add_argument('--remote-port', action="store", dest="remote_
port", type=int, default=80)
    given_args = parser.parse_args()
    local_host, remote_host = given_args.local_host, given_args.
remote_host
    local_port, remote_port = given_args.local_port, given_args.
remote_port
    print "Starting port forwarding local %s:%s => remote %s:%s" %
(local_host, local_port, remote_host, remote_port)
    PortForwarder(local_host, local_port, remote_host, remote_port)
    asyncore.loop()
```

If you run this script, it will show the following output:

```
$ python 3_1_port_forwarding.py --local-port=8800
Starting port forwarding local localhost:8800 => remote www.google.com:80
```

Now, open your browser and visit `http://localhost:8800`. This will take you to the Google home page and the script will print something similar to the following command:

```
Connected to: ('127.0.0.1', 38557)
```

The following screenshot shows the forwarding a local port to a remote host:

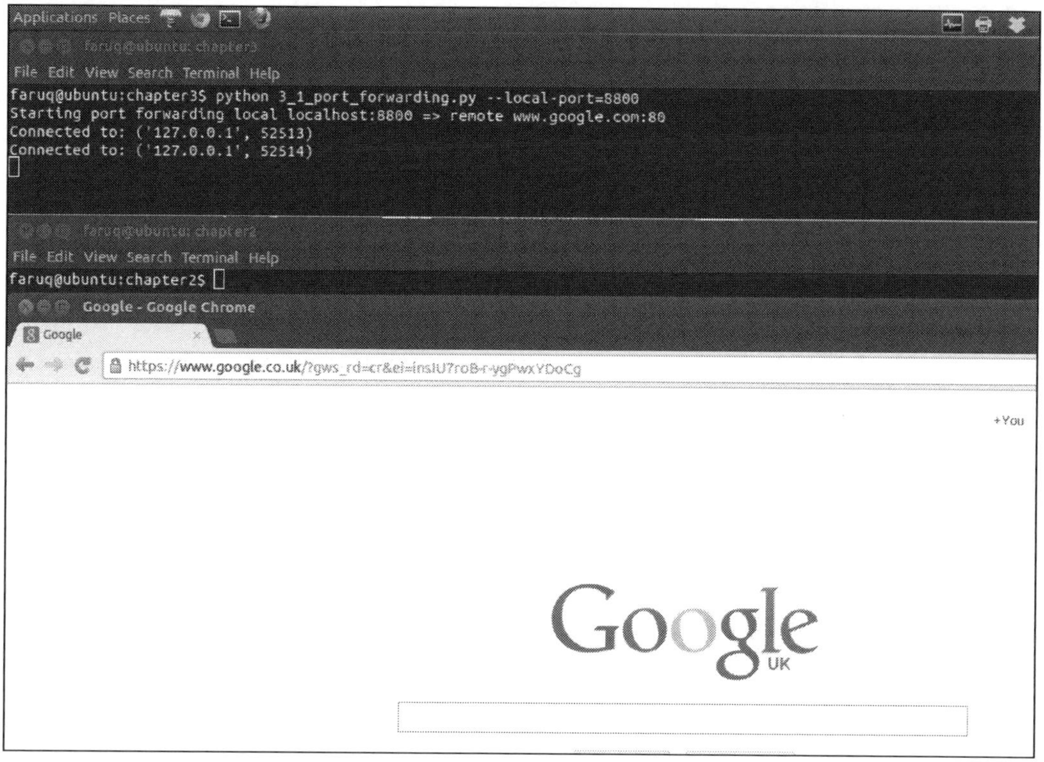

How it works...

We created a port forwarding class, `PortForwarder subclassed`, from `asyncore.dispatcher`, which wraps around the socket object. It provides a few additional helpful functions when certain events occur, for example, when the connection is successful or a client is connected to a server socket. You have the choice of overriding the set of methods defined in this class. In our case, we only override the `handle_accept()` method.

Two other classes have been derived from `asyncore.dispatcher`. The `Receiver` class handles the incoming client requests and the `Sender` class takes this `Receiver` instance and processes the sent data to the clients. As you can see, these two classes override the `handle_read()`, `handle_write()`, and `writeable()` methods to facilitate the bi-directional communication between the remote host and local client.

In summary, the `PortForwarder` class takes the incoming client request in a local socket and passes this to the `Sender` class instance, which in turn uses the `Receiver` class instance to initiate a bi-directional communication with a remote server in the specified port.

Pinging hosts on the network with ICMP

An ICMP ping is the most common type of network scanning you have ever encountered. It is very easy to open a command-line prompt or terminal and type `ping www.google.com`. How difficult is that from inside a Python program? This recipe shows you an example of a Python ping.

Getting ready

You need the superuser or administrator privilege to run this recipe on your machine.

How to do it...

You can lazily write a Python script that calls the system ping command-line tool, as follows:

```
import subprocess
import shlex

command_line = "ping -c 1 www.google.com"
args = shlex.split(command_line)
try:
      subprocess.check_call(args,stdout=subprocess.PIPE,\
stderr=subprocess.PIPE)
    print "Google web server is up!"
except subprocess.CalledProcessError:
    print "Failed to get ping."
```

However, in many circumstances, the system's ping executable may not be available or may be inaccessible. In this case, we need a pure Python script to do that ping. Note that this script needs to be run as a superuser or administrator.

Listing 3.2 shows the ICMP ping, as follows:

```
#!/usr/bin/env python
# Python Network Programming Cookbook -- Chapter - 3
# This program is optimized for Python 2.7.
# It may run on any other version with/without modifications.

import os
import argparse
import socket
import struct
import select
import time
```

```
ICMP_ECHO_REQUEST = 8 # Platform specific
DEFAULT_TIMEOUT = 2
DEFAULT_COUNT = 4

class Pinger(object):
    """ Pings to a host -- the Pythonic way"""
    def __init__(self, target_host, count=DEFAULT_COUNT,
timeout=DEFAULT_TIMEOUT):
        self.target_host = target_host
        self.count = count
        self.timeout = timeout
    def do_checksum(self, source_string):
        """  Verify the packet integritity """
        sum = 0
        max_count = (len(source_string)/2)*2
        count = 0
        while count < max_count:
            val = ord(source_string[count + 1])*256 + ord(source_
string[count])
            sum = sum + val
            sum = sum & 0xffffffff
            count = count + 2
        if max_count<len(source_string):
            sum = sum + ord(source_string[len(source_string) - 1])
            sum = sum & 0xffffffff
        sum = (sum >> 16)  +  (sum & 0xffff)
        sum = sum + (sum >> 16)
        answer = ~sum
        answer = answer & 0xffff
        answer = answer >> 8 | (answer << 8 & 0xff00)
        return answer

    def receive_pong(self, sock, ID, timeout):
        """
        Receive ping from the socket.
        """
        time_remaining = timeout
        while True:
            start_time = time.time()
            readable = select.select([sock], [], [], time_remaining)
            time_spent = (time.time() - start_time)
            if readable[0] == []: # Timeout
                return

            time_received = time.time()
            recv_packet, addr = sock.recvfrom(1024)
            icmp_header = recv_packet[20:28]
```

```
            type, code, checksum, packet_ID, sequence = struct.unpack(
                "bbHHh", icmp_header
            )
            if packet_ID == ID:
                bytes_In_double = struct.calcsize("d")
                time_sent = struct.unpack("d", recv_packet[28:28 +
bytes_In_double])[0]
                return time_received - time_sent

            time_remaining = time_remaining - time_spent
            if time_remaining <= 0:
                return
```

We need a `send_ping()` method that will send the data of a ping request to the target host. Also, this will call the `do_checksum()` method for checking the integrity of the ping data, as follows:

```
    def send_ping(self, sock,  ID):
        """
        Send ping to the target host
        """
        target_addr  =  socket.gethostbyname(self.target_host)
        my_checksum = 0
        # Create a dummy header with a 0 checksum.
        header = struct.pack("bbHHh", ICMP_ECHO_REQUEST, 0, my_
checksum, ID, 1)
        bytes_In_double = struct.calcsize("d")
        data = (192 - bytes_In_double) * "Q"
        data = struct.pack("d", time.time()) + data
        # Get the checksum on the data and the dummy header.
        my_checksum = self.do_checksum(header + data)
        header = struct.pack(
            "bbHHh", ICMP_ECHO_REQUEST, 0, socket.htons(my_checksum),
ID, 1
        )
        packet = header + data
        sock.sendto(packet, (target_addr, 1))
```

Let us define another method called `ping_once()` that makes a single ping call to the target host. It creates a raw ICMP socket by passing the ICMP protocol to `socket()`. The exception handling code takes care if the script is not run by a superuser or if any other socket error occurs. Let's take a look at the following code:

```
    def ping_once(self):
        """
        Returns the delay (in seconds) or none on timeout.
        """
        icmp = socket.getprotobyname("icmp")
```

```
        try:
            sock = socket.socket(socket.AF_INET, socket.SOCK_RAW,
icmp)
        except socket.error, (errno, msg):
            if errno == 1:
                # Not superuser, so operation not permitted
                msg +=  "ICMP messages can only be sent from root user
processes"
                raise socket.error(msg)
        except Exception, e:
            print "Exception: %s" %(e)
        my_ID = os.getpid() & 0xFFFF
        self.send_ping(sock, my_ID)
        delay = self.receive_pong(sock, my_ID, self.timeout)
        sock.close()
        return delay
```

The main executive method of this class is `ping()`. It runs a `for` loop inside which the `ping_once()` method is called count times and receives a delay in the ping response in seconds. If no delay is returned, that means the ping has failed. Let's take a look at the following code:

```
    def ping(self):
        """
        Run the ping process
        """
        for i in xrange(self.count):
            print "Ping to %s..." % self.target_host,
            try:
                delay  =  self.ping_once()
            except socket.gaierror, e:
                print "Ping failed. (socket error: '%s')" % e[1]
                break
            if delay  ==  None:
               print "Ping failed. (timeout within %ssec.)" % \  \
                     self.timeout
            else:
                delay  =  delay * 1000
                print "Get pong in %0.4fms" % delay

if __name__ == '__main__':
    parser = argparse.ArgumentParser(description='Python ping')
    parser.add_argument('--target-host', action="store", dest="target_
host", required=True)
    given_args = parser.parse_args()
    target_host = given_args.target_host
    pinger = Pinger(target_host=target_host)
    pinger.ping()
```

This script shows the following output. This has been run with the superuser privilege:

```
$ sudo python 3_2_ping_remote_host.py --target-host=www.google.com
Ping to www.google.com... Get pong in 7.6921ms
Ping to www.google.com... Get pong in 7.1061ms
Ping to www.google.com... Get pong in 8.9211ms
Ping to www.google.com... Get pong in 7.9899ms
```

How it works...

A `Pinger` class has been constructed to define a few useful methods. The class initializes with a few user-defined or default inputs, which are as follows:

- `target_host`: This is the target host to ping
- `count`: This is how many times to do the ping
- `timeout`: This is the value that determines when to end an unfinished ping operation

The `send_ping()` method gets the DNS hostname of the target host and creates an `ICMP_ECHO_REQUEST` packet using the `struct` module. It's necessary to check the data integrity of the method using the `do_checksum()` method. It takes the source string and manipulates it to produce a proper checksum. On the receiving end, the `receive_pong()` method waits for a response until the timeout occurs or receives the response. It captures the ICMP response header and then compares the packet ID and calculates the delay in the request and response cycle.

Waiting for a remote network service

Sometimes, during the recovery of a network service, it might be useful to run a script to check when the server is online again.

How to do it...

We can write a client that will wait for a particular network service forever or for a timeout. In this example, by default, we would like to check when a web server is up in localhost. If you specified some other remote host or port, that information will be used instead.

Listing 3.3 shows waiting for a remote network service, as follows:

```
#!/usr/bin/env python
# Python Network Programming Cookbook -- Chapter - 3
# This program is optimized for Python 2.7.
# It may run on any other version with/without modifications.
```

```
import argparse
import socket
import errno
from time import time as now

DEFAULT_TIMEOUT = 120
DEFAULT_SERVER_HOST = 'localhost'
DEFAULT_SERVER_PORT = 80

class NetServiceChecker(object):
    """ Wait for a network service to come online"""
    def __init__(self, host, port, timeout=DEFAULT_TIMEOUT):
        self.host = host
        self.port = port
        self.timeout = timeout
        self.sock = socket.socket(socket.AF_INET, socket.SOCK_STREAM)

    def end_wait(self):
        self.sock.close()

    def check(self):
        """ Check the service """
        if self.timeout:
            end_time = now() + self.timeout

        while True:
            try:
                if self.timeout:
                    next_timeout = end_time - now()
                    if next_timeout < 0:
                        return False
                    else:
                        print "setting socket next timeout %ss"\
                       %round(next_timeout)
                        self.sock.settimeout(next_timeout)
                self.sock.connect((self.host, self.port))
            # handle exceptions
            except socket.timeout, err:
                if self.timeout:
                    return False
            except socket.error, err:
                print "Exception: %s" %err
            else: # if all goes well
                self.end_wait()
```

```
                return True

if __name__ == '__main__':
    parser = argparse.ArgumentParser(description='Wait for Network
Service')
    parser.add_argument('--host', action="store", dest="host",
default=DEFAULT_SERVER_HOST)
    parser.add_argument('--port', action="store", dest="port",
type=int, default=DEFAULT_SERVER_PORT)
    parser.add_argument('--timeout', action="store", dest="timeout",
type=int, default=DEFAULT_TIMEOUT)
    given_args = parser.parse_args()
    host, port, timeout = given_args.host, given_args.port, given_
args.timeout
    service_checker = NetServiceChecker(host, port, timeout=timeout)
    print "Checking for network service %s:%s ..." %(host, port)
    if service_checker.check():
        print "Service is available again!"
```

If a web server, such as Apache, is running on your machine, this script will show the following output:

```
$ python 3_3_wait_for_remote_service.py
Waiting for network service localhost:80 ...
setting socket next timeout 120.0s
Service is available again!
```

Now, stop the Apache process, run this script, and restart Apache again. The output pattern will be different. On my machine, the following output pattern was found:

```
Exception: [Errno 103] Software caused connection abort
setting socket next timeout 104.189137936
Exception: [Errno 111] Connection refused
setting socket next timeout 104.186291933
Exception: [Errno 103] Software caused connection abort
setting socket next timeout 104.186164856
Service is available again!
```

The following screenshot shows the waiting for an active Apache web server process:

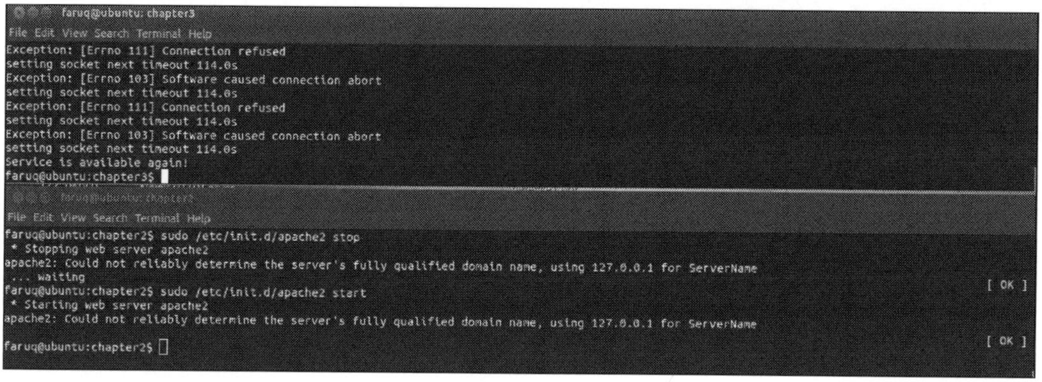

How it works...

The preceding script uses the `argparse` module to take the user input and process the hostname, port, and timeout, that is how long our script will wait for the desired network service. It launches an instance of the `NetServiceChecker` class and calls the `check()` method. This method calculates the final end time of waiting and uses the socket's `settimeout()` method to control each round's end time, that is `next_timeout`. It then uses the socket's `connect()` method to test if the desired network service is available until the socket timeout occurs. This method also catches the socket timeout error and checks the socket timeout against the timeout values given by the user.

Enumerating interfaces on your machine

If you need to list the network interfaces present on your machine, it is not very complicated in Python. There are a couple of third-party libraries out there that can do this job in a few lines. However, let's see how this is done using a pure socket call.

Getting ready

You need to run this recipe on a Linux box. To get the list of available interfaces, you can execute the following command:

```
$ /sbin/ifconfig
```

How to do it...

Listing 3.4 shows how to list the networking interfaces, as follows:

```
#!/usr/bin/env python
# Python Network Programming Cookbook -- Chapter - 3
# This program is optimized for Python 2.7.
# It may run on any other version with/without modifications.
import sys
import socket
import fcntl
import struct
import array

SIOCGIFCONF = 0x8912 #from C library sockios.h
STUCT_SIZE_32 = 32
STUCT_SIZE_64 = 40
PLATFORM_32_MAX_NUMBER =  2**32
DEFAULT_INTERFACES = 8


def list_interfaces():
    interfaces = []
    max_interfaces = DEFAULT_INTERFACES
    is_64bits = sys.maxsize > PLATFORM_32_MAX_NUMBER
    struct_size = STUCT_SIZE_64 if is_64bits else STUCT_SIZE_32
    sock = socket.socket(socket.AF_INET, socket.SOCK_DGRAM)
    while True:
        bytes = max_interfaces * struct_size
        interface_names = array.array('B', '\0' * bytes)
        sock_info = fcntl.ioctl(
            sock.fileno(),
            SIOCGIFCONF,
            struct.pack('iL', bytes,interface_names.buffer_info()[0])
        )
        outbytes = struct.unpack('iL', sock_info)[0]
        if outbytes == bytes:
            max_interfaces *= 2
        else:
            break
    namestr = interface_names.tostring()
    for i in range(0, outbytes, struct_size):
        interfaces.append((namestr[i:i+16].split('\0', 1)[0]))
    return interfaces

if __name__ == '__main__':
    interfaces = list_interfaces()
    print "This machine has %s network interfaces: %s."
%(len(interfaces), interface)
```

The preceding script will list the network interfaces, as shown in the following output:

```
$ python 3_4_list_network_interfaces.py
This machine has 2 network interfaces: ['lo', 'eth0'].
```

How it works...

This recipe code uses a low-level socket feature to find out the interfaces present on the system. The single `list_interfaces()` method creates a socket object and finds the network interface information from manipulating this object. It does so by making a call to the `fnctl` module's `ioctl()` method. The `fnctl` module interfaces with some Unix routines, for example, `fnctl()`. This interface performs an I/O control operation on the underlying file descriptor socket, which is obtained by calling the `fileno()` method of the socket object.

The additional parameter of the `ioctl()` method includes the `SIOCGIFADDR` constant defined in the C socket library and a data structure produced by the `struct` module's `pack()` function. The memory address specified by a data structure is modified as a result of the `ioctl()` call. In this case, the `interface_names` variable holds this information. After unpacking the `sock_info` return value of the `ioctl()` call, the number of network interfaces is increased twice if the size of the data suggests it. This is done in a `while` loop to discover all interfaces if our initial interface count assumption is not correct.

The names of interfaces are extracted from the string format of the `interface_names` variable. It reads specific fields of that variable and appends the values in the interfaces' list. At the end of the `list_interfaces()` function, this is returned.

Finding the IP address for a specific interface on your machine

Finding the IP address of a particular network interface may be needed from your Python network application.

Getting ready

This recipe is prepared exclusively for a Linux box. There are some Python modules specially designed to bring similar functionalities on Windows and Mac platforms. For example, see `http://sourceforge.net/projects/pywin32/` for Windows-specific implementation.

How to do it...

You can use the `fnctl` module to query the IP address on your machine.

Listing 3.5 shows us how to find the IP address for a specific interface on your machine, as follows:

```
#!/usr/bin/env python
# Python Network Programming Cookbook -- Chapter - 3
# This program is optimized for Python 2.7.
# It may run on any other version with/without modifications.

import argparse
import sys
import socket
import fcntl
import struct
import array

def get_ip_address(ifname):
    s = socket.socket(socket.AF_INET, socket.SOCK_DGRAM)
    return socket.inet_ntoa(fcntl.ioctl(
        s.fileno(),
        0x8915,  # SIOCGIFADDR
        struct.pack('256s', ifname[:15])
    )[20:24])

if __name__ == '__main__':
    #interfaces =  list_interfaces()
    parser = argparse.ArgumentParser(description='Python networking
utils')
    parser.add_argument('--ifname', action="store", dest="ifname",
required=True)
    given_args = parser.parse_args()
    ifname = given_args.ifname
    print "Interface [%s] --> IP: %s" %(ifname, get_ip_
address(ifname))
```

The output of this script is shown in one line, as follows:

```
$ python 3_5_get_interface_ip_address.py --ifname=eth0
Interface [eth0] --> IP: 10.0.2.15
```

How it works...

This recipe is similar to the previous one. The preceding script takes a command-line argument: the name of the network interface whose IP address is to be known. The `get_ip_address()` function creates a socket object and calls the `fnctl.ioctl()` function to query on that object about IP information. Note that the `socket.inet_ntoa()` function converts the binary data to a human-readable string in a dotted format as we are familiar with it.

Finding whether an interface is up on your machine

If you have multiple network interfaces on your machine, before doing any work on a particular interface, you would like to know the status of that network interface, for example, if the interface is actually up. This makes sure that you route your command to active interfaces.

Getting ready

This recipe is written for a Linux machine. So, this script will not run on a Windows or Mac host. In this recipe, we use `nmap`, a famous network scanning tool. You can find more about `nmap` from its website `http://nmap.org/`.

You also need the `python-nmap` module to run this recipe. This can be installed by `pip`, as follows:

```
$ pip install python-nmap
```

How to do it...

We can create a socket object and get the IP address of that interface. Then, we can use any of the scanning techniques to probe the interface status.

Listing 3.6 shows the detect network interface status, as follows:

```
#!/usr/bin/env python
# Python Network Programming Cookbook -- Chapter - 3
# This program is optimized for Python 2.7.
# It may run on any other version with/without modifications.

import argparse
import socket
import struct
import fcntl
import nmap
SAMPLE_PORTS = '21-23'

def get_interface_status(ifname):
    sock = socket.socket(socket.AF_INET, socket.SOCK_DGRAM)
    ip_address = socket.inet_ntoa(fcntl.ioctl(
        sock.fileno(),
        0x8915, #SIOCGIFADDR, C socket library sockios.h
        struct.pack('256s', ifname[:15])
    )[20:24])
```

```
        nm = nmap.PortScanner()
        nm.scan(ip_address, SAMPLE_PORTS)
        return nm[ip_address].state()

    if __name__ == '__main__':
        parser = argparse.ArgumentParser(description='Python networking
    utils')
        parser.add_argument('--ifname', action="store", dest="ifname",
    required=True)
        given_args = parser.parse_args()
        ifname = given_args.ifname
        print "Interface [%s] is: %s" %(ifname, get_interface_
    status(ifname))
```

If you run this script to inquire the status of the `eth0` status, it will show something similar to the following output:

```
$ python 3_6_find_network_interface_status.py --ifname=eth0
Interface [eth0] is: up
```

How it works...

The recipe takes the interface's name from the command line and passes it to the `get_interface_status()` function. This function finds the IP address of that interface by manipulating a UDP socket object.

This recipe needs the `nmap` third-party module. We can install that PyPI using the `pip` install command. The `nmap` scanning instance, `nm`, has been created by calling `PortScanner()`. An initial scan to a local IP address gives us the status of the associated network interface.

Detecting inactive machines on your network

If you have been given a list of IP addresses of a few machines on your network and you are asked to write a script to find out which hosts are inactive periodically, you would want to create a network scanner type program without installing anything on the target host computers.

Getting ready

This recipe requires installing the Scapy library (> 2.2), which can be obtained at `http://www.secdev.org/projects/scapy/files/scapy-latest.zip`.

How to do it...

We can use Scapy, a mature network-analyzing, third-party library, to launch an ICMP scan. Since we would like to do it periodically, we need Python's `sched` module to schedule the scanning tasks.

Listing 3.7 shows us how to detect inactive machines, as follows:

```
#!/usr/bin/env python
# Python Network Programming Cookbook -- Chapter - 3
# This program is optimized for Python 2.7.
# It may run on any other version with/without modifications.
# This recipe requires scapy-2.2.0 or higher

import argparse
import time
import sched
from scapy.all import sr, srp, IP, UDP, ICMP, TCP, ARP, Ether
RUN_FREQUENCY = 10
scheduler = sched.scheduler(time.time, time.sleep)

def detect_inactive_hosts(scan_hosts):
    """
    Scans the network to find scan_hosts are live or dead
    scan_hosts can be like 10.0.2.2-4 to cover range.
    See Scapy docs for specifying targets.
    """
    global scheduler
    scheduler.enter(RUN_FREQUENCY, 1, detect_inactive_hosts, (scan_
hosts, ))
    inactive_hosts = []
    try:
        ans, unans = sr(IP(dst=scan_hosts)/ICMP(),retry=0, timeout=1)
        ans.summary(lambda(s,r) : r.sprintf("%IP.src% is alive"))
        for inactive in unans:
            print "%s is inactive" %inactive.dst
            inactive_hosts.append(inactive.dst)
        print "Total %d hosts are inactive" %(len(inactive_hosts))
    except KeyboardInterrupt:
        exit(0)
if __name__ == "__main__":
    parser = argparse.ArgumentParser(description='Python networking
utils')
    parser.add_argument('--scan-hosts', action="store", dest="scan_
hosts", required=True)
    given_args = parser.parse_args()
    scan_hosts = given_args.scan_hosts
    scheduler.enter(1, 1, detect_inactive_hosts, (scan_hosts, ))
    scheduler.run()
```

The output of this script will be something like the following command:

```
$ sudo python 3_7_detect_inactive_machines.py --scan-hosts=10.0.2.2-4
Begin emission:
.*...Finished to send 3 packets.
.
Received 6 packets, got 1 answers, remaining 2 packets
10.0.2.2 is alive
10.0.2.4 is inactive
10.0.2.3 is inactive
Total 2 hosts are inactive
Begin emission:
*.Finished to send 3 packets.
Received 3 packets, got 1 answers, remaining 2 packets
10.0.2.2 is alive
10.0.2.4 is inactive
10.0.2.3 is inactive
Total 2 hosts are inactive
```

How it works...

The preceding script first takes a list of network hosts, `scan_hosts`, from the command line. It then creates a schedule to launch the `detect_inactive_hosts()` function after a one-second delay. The target function takes the `scan_hosts` argument and calls Scapy's `sr()` function.

This function schedules itself to rerun after every 10 seconds by calling the `schedule.enter()` function once again. This way, we run this scanning task periodically.

Scapy's `sr()` scanning function takes an IP, protocol and some scan-control information. In this case, the `IP()` method passes `scan_hosts` as the destination hosts to scan, and the protocol is specified as ICMP. This can also be TCP or UDP. We do not specify a retry and one-second timeout to run this script faster. However, you can experiment with the options that suit you.

The scanning `sr()`function returns the hosts that answer and those that don't as a tuple. We check the hosts that don't answer, build a list, and print that information.

Performing a basic IPC using connected sockets (socketpair)

Sometimes, two scripts need to communicate some information between themselves via two processes. In Unix/Linux, there's a concept of connected socket, of `socketpair`. We can experiment with this here.

Getting ready

This recipe is designed for a Unix/Linux host. Windows/Mac is not suitable for running this one.

How to do it...

We use a `test_socketpair()` function to wrap a few lines that test the socket's `socketpair()` function.

List 3.8 shows an example of `socketpair`, as follows:

```
#!/usr/bin/env python
# Python Network Programming Cookbook -- Chapter - 3
# This program is optimized for Python 2.7.
# It may run on any other version with/without modifications.

import socket
import os

BUFSIZE = 1024

def test_socketpair():
    """ Test Unix socketpair"""
    parent, child = socket.socketpair()

    pid = os.fork()
    try:
        if pid:
            print "@Parent, sending message..."
            child.close()
            parent.sendall("Hello from parent!")
            response = parent.recv(BUFSIZE)
            print "Response from child:", response
            parent.close()

        else:
            print "@Child, waiting for message from parent"
```

```
            parent.close()
            message = child.recv(BUFSIZE)
            print "Message from parent:", message
            child.sendall("Hello from child!!")
            child.close()
    except Exception, err:
        print "Error: %s" %err

if __name__ == '__main__':
    test_socketpair()
```

The output from the preceding script is as follows:

```
$ python 3_8_ipc_using_socketpairs.py
@Parent, sending message...
@Child, waiting for message from parent
Message from parent: Hello from parent!
Response from child: Hello from child!!
```

How it works...

The `socket.socketpair()` function simply returns two connected socket objects. In our case, we can say that one is a parent and another is a child. We fork another process via a `os.fork()` call. This returns the process ID of the parent. In each process, the other process' socket is closed first and then a message is exchanged via a `sendall()` method call on the process's socket. The try-except block prints any error in case of any kind of exception.

Performing IPC using Unix domain sockets

Unix domain sockets (**UDS**) are sometimes used as a convenient way to communicate between two processes. As in Unix, everything is conceptually a file. If you need an example of such an IPC action, this can be useful.

How to do it...

We launch a UDS server that binds to a filesystem path, and a UDS client uses the same path to communicate with the server.

Listing 3.9a shows a Unix domain socket server, as follows:

```
#!/usr/bin/env python
# Python Network Programming Cookbook -- Chapter - 3
# This program is optimized for Python 2.7.
# It may run on any other version with/without modifications.
```

```
import socket
import os
import time

SERVER_PATH = "/tmp/python_unix_socket_server"

def run_unix_domain_socket_server():
    if os.path.exists(SERVER_PATH):
        os.remove( SERVER_PATH )

    print "starting unix domain socket server."
    server = socket.socket( socket.AF_UNIX, socket.SOCK_DGRAM )
    server.bind(SERVER_PATH)

    print "Listening on path: %s" %SERVER_PATH
    while True:
        datagram = server.recv( 1024 )
        if not datagram:
            break
        else:
            print "-" * 20
            print datagram
        if "DONE" == datagram:
            break
    print "-" * 20
    print "Server is shutting down now..."
    server.close()
    os.remove(SERVER_PATH)
    print "Server shutdown and path removed."

if __name__ == '__main__':
    run_unix_domain_socket_server()
```

Listing 3.9b shows a UDS client, as follows:

```
#!/usr/bin/env python
# Python Network Programming Cookbook -- Chapter - 3
# This program is optimized for Python 2.7.
# It may run on any other version with/without modifications.

import socket
import sys

SERVER_PATH = "/tmp/python_unix_socket_server"

def run_unix_domain_socket_client():
    """ Run "a Unix domain socket client """
    sock = socket.socket(socket.AF_UNIX, socket.SOCK_DGRAM)
```

```
        # Connect the socket to the path where the server is listening
        server_address = SERVER_PATH
        print "connecting to %s" % server_address
        try:
            sock.connect(server_address)
        except socket.error, msg:
            print >>sys.stderr, msg
            sys.exit(1)

        try:
            message = "This is the message.  This will be echoed back!"
            print  "Sending [%s]" %message
            sock.sendall(message)
            amount_received = 0
            amount_expected = len(message)

            while amount_received < amount_expected:
                data = sock.recv(16)
                amount_received += len(data)
                print >>sys.stderr, "Received [%s]" % data

        finally:
            print "Closing client"
            sock.close()

    if __name__ == '__main__':
        run_unix_domain_socket_client()
```

The server output is as follows:

```
$ python 3_9a_unix_domain_socket_server.py
starting unix domain socket server.
Listening on path: /tmp/python_unix_socket_server
--------------------
This is the message.  This will be echoed back!
```

The client output is as follows:

```
$ python 3_9b_unix_domain_socket_client.py
connecting to /tmp/python_unix_socket_server
Sending [This is the message.  This will be echoed back!]
```

How it works...

A common path is defined for a UDS client/server to interact. Both the client and server use the same path to connect and listen to.

In a server code, we remove the path if it exists from the previous run of this script. It then creates a Unix datagram socket and binds it to the specified path. It then listens for incoming connections. In the data processing loop, it uses the `recv()` method to get data from the client and prints that information on screen.

The client-side code simply opens a Unix datagram socket and connects to the shared server address. It sends a message to the server using `sendall()`. It then waits for the message to be echoed back to itself and prints that message.

Finding out if your Python supports IPv6 sockets

IP version 6 or IPv6 is increasingly adopted by the industry to build newer applications. In case you would like to write an IPv6 application, the first thing you'd like to know is if your machine supports IPv6. This can be done from the Linux/Unix command line, as follows:

```
$ cat /proc/net/if_inet6
00000000000000000000000000000001 01 80 10 80        lo
fe800000000000000a0027fffe950d1a 02 40 20 80      eth0
```

From your Python script, you can also check if the IPv6 support is present on your machine, and Python is installed with that support.

Getting ready

For this recipe, use `pip` to install a Python third-party library, `netifaces`, as follows:

```
$ pip install   netifaces
```

How to do it...

We can use a third-party library, `netifaces`, to find out if there is IPv6 support on your machine. We can call the `interfaces()` function from this library to list all interfaces present in the system.

Listing 3.10 shows the Python IPv6 support checker, as follows:

```
#!/usr/bin/env python
# Python Network Programming Cookbook -- Chapter - 3
# This program is optimized for Python 2.7.
```

```
# It may run on any other version with/without modifications.
# This program depends on Python module netifaces => 0.8
import socket
import argparse
import netifaces as ni

def inspect_ipv6_support():
    """ Find the ipv6 address"""
    print "IPV6 support built into Python: %s" %socket.has_ipv6
    ipv6_addr = {}
    for interface in ni.interfaces():
        all_addresses = ni.ifaddresses(interface)
        print "Interface %s:" %interface
        for family,addrs in all_addresses.iteritems():
            fam_name = ni.address_families[family]
            print '  Address family: %s' % fam_name
            for addr in addrs:
                if fam_name == 'AF_INET6':
                    ipv6_addr[interface] = addr['addr']
                print     '    Address   : %s' % addr['addr']
                nmask = addr.get('netmask', None)
                if nmask:
                    print '    Netmask   : %s' % nmask
                bcast = addr.get('broadcast', None)
                if bcast:
                    print '    Broadcast: %s' % bcast
    if ipv6_addr:
        print "Found IPv6 address: %s" %ipv6_addr
    else:
        print "No IPv6 interface found!"

if __name__ == '__main__':
    inspect_ipv6_support()
```

The output from this script will be as follows:

```
$ python 3_10_check_ipv6_support.py
IPV6 support built into Python: True
Interface lo:
  Address family: AF_PACKET
    Address   : 00:00:00:00:00:00
  Address family: AF_INET
    Address   : 127.0.0.1
```

```
    Netmask  : 255.0.0.0
  Address family: AF_INET6
    Address  : ::1
    Netmask  : ffff:ffff:ffff:ffff:ffff:ffff:ffff:ffff
Interface eth0:
  Address family: AF_PACKET
    Address  : 08:00:27:95:0d:1a
    Broadcast: ff:ff:ff:ff:ff:ff
  Address family: AF_INET
    Address  : 10.0.2.15
    Netmask  : 255.255.255.0
    Broadcast: 10.0.2.255
  Address family: AF_INET6
    Address  : fe80::a00:27ff:fe95:d1a
    Netmask  : ffff:ffff:ffff:ffff::
Found IPv6 address: {'lo': '::1', 'eth0': 'fe80::a00:27ff:fe95:d1a'}
```

The following screenshot shows the interaction between the IPv6 client and server:

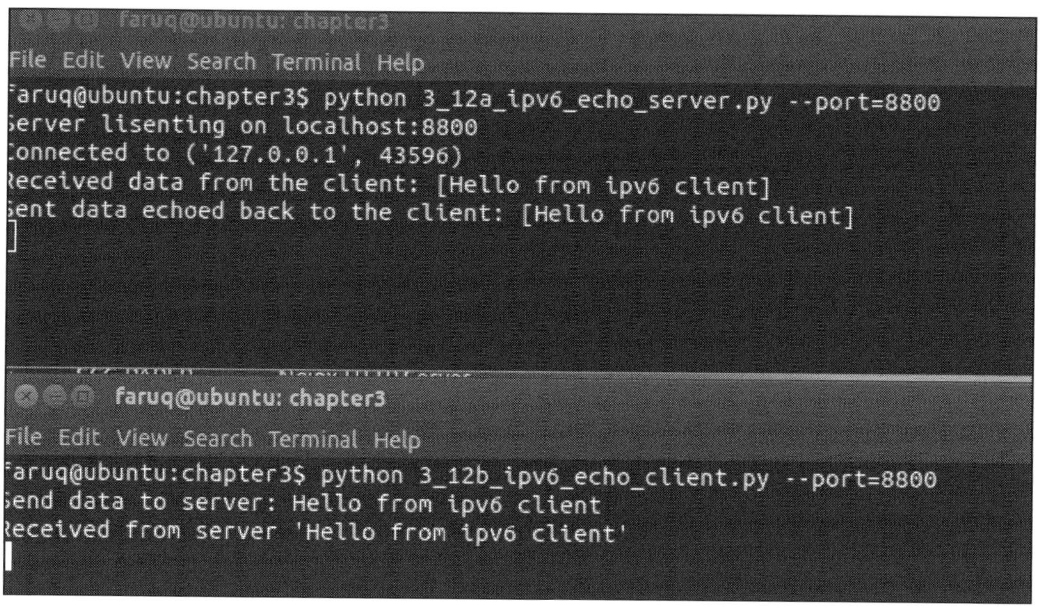

How it works...

The IPv6 support checker function, `inspect_ipv6_support()`, first checks if Python is built with IPv6 using `socket.has_ipv6`. Next, we call the `interfaces()` function from the `netifaces` module. This gives us the list of all interfaces. If we call the `ifaddresses()` method by passing a network interface to it, we can get all the IP addresses of this interface. We then extract various IP-related information, such as protocol family, address, netmask, and broadcast address. Then, the address of a network interface has been added to the `IPv6_address` dictionary if its protocol family matches `AF_INET6`.

Extracting an IPv6 prefix from an IPv6 address

In your IPv6 application, you need to dig out the IPv6 address for getting the prefix information. Note that the upper 64-bits of an IPv6 address are represented from a global routing prefix plus a subnet ID, as defined in RFC 3513. A general prefix (for example, /48) holds a short prefix based on which a number of longer, more specific prefixes (for example, /64) can be defined. A Python script can be very helpful in generating the prefix information.

How to do it...

We can use the `netifaces` and `netaddr` third-party libraries to find out the IPv6 prefix information for a given IPv6 address, as follows:

```
#!/usr/bin/env python
# Python Network Programming Cookbook -- Chapter - 3
# This program is optimized for Python 2.7.
# It may run on any other version with/without modifications.

import socket
import netifaces as ni
import netaddr as na

def extract_ipv6_info():
    """ Extracts IPv6 information"""
    print "IPV6 support built into Python: %s" %socket.has_ipv6
    for interface in ni.interfaces():
        all_addresses = ni.ifaddresses(interface)
        print "Interface %s:" %interface
        for family,addrs in all_addresses.iteritems():
            fam_name = ni.address_families[family]
            #print '  Address family: %s' % fam_name
            for addr in addrs:
                if fam_name == 'AF_INET6':
```

```
                    addr = addr['addr']
                    has_eth_string = addr.split("%eth")
                    if has_eth_string:
        addr = addr.split("%eth")[0]
        print "    IP Address: %s" %na.IPNetwork(addr)
        print "    IP Version: %s" %na.IPNetwork(addr).version
        print "    IP Prefix length: %s" %na.IPNetwork(addr).prefixlen
        print "    Network: %s" %na.IPNetwork(addr).network
        print "    Broadcast: %s" %na.IPNetwork(addr).broadcast
if __name__ == '__main__':
    extract_ipv6_info()
```

The output from this script is as follows:

```
$ python 3_11_extract_ipv6_prefix.py
IPV6 support built into Python: True
Interface lo:
    IP Address: ::1/128
    IP Version: 6
    IP Prefix length: 128
    Network: ::1
    Broadcast: ::1
Interface eth0:
    IP Address: fe80::a00:27ff:fe95:d1a/128
    IP Version: 6
    IP Prefix length: 128
    Network: fe80::a00:27ff:fe95:d1a
    Broadcast: fe80::a00:27ff:fe95:d1a
```

How it works...

Python's `netifaces` module gives us the network interface IPv6 address. It uses the `interfaces()` and `ifaddresses()` functions for doing this. The `netaddr` module is particularly helpful to manipulate a network address. It has a `IPNetwork()` class that provides us with an address, IPv4 or IPv6, and computes the prefix, network, and broadcast addresses. Here, we find this information class instance's version, prefixlen, and network and broadcast attributes.

Writing an IPv6 echo client/server

You need to write an IPv6 compliant server or client and wonder what could be the differences between an IPv6 compliant server or client and its IPv4 counterpart.

How to do it...

We use the same approach as writing an echo client/server using IPv6. The only major difference is how the socket is created using IPv6 information.

Listing 12a shows an IPv6 echo server, as follows:

```
#!/usr/bin/env python
# Python Network Programming Cookbook -- Chapter - 3
# This program is optimized for Python 2.7.
# It may run on any other version with/without modifications.

import argparse
import socket
import sys

HOST = 'localhost'

def echo_server(port, host=HOST):
    """Echo server using IPv6 """
    for res in socket.getaddrinfo(host, port, socket.AF_UNSPEC,
            socket.SOCK_STREAM, 0, socket.AI_PASSIVE):
        af, socktype, proto, canonname, sa = res
        try:
            sock = socket.socket(af, socktype, proto)
        except socket.error, err:
            print "Error: %s" %err

        try:
            sock.bind(sa)
            sock.listen(1)
            print "Server listening on %s:%s" %(host, port)
        except socket.error, msg:
            sock.close()
            continue
        break
        sys.exit(1)
    conn, addr = sock.accept()
    print 'Connected to', addr
    while True:
        data = conn.recv(1024)
```

```
            print "Received data from the client: [%s]" %data
            if not data: break
            conn.send(data)
            print "Sent data echoed back to the client: [%s]" %data
        conn.close()

if __name__ == '__main__':
    parser = argparse.ArgumentParser(description='IPv6 Socket Server
Example')
    parser.add_argument('--port', action="store", dest="port",
type=int, required=True)
    given_args = parser.parse_args()
    port = given_args.port
    echo_server(port)
```

Listing 12b shows an IPv6 echo client, as follows:

```
#!/usr/bin/env python
# Python Network Programming Cookbook -- Chapter - 3
# This program is optimized for Python 2.7.

# It may run on any other version with/without modifications.

import argparse
import socket
import sys

HOST = 'localhost'
BUFSIZE = 1024

def ipv6_echo_client(port, host=HOST):
    for res in socket.getaddrinfo(host, port, socket.AF_UNSPEC,
socket.SOCK_STREAM):
        af, socktype, proto, canonname, sa = res
        try:
            sock = socket.socket(af, socktype, proto)
        except socket.error, err:
            print "Error:%s" %err
        try:
            sock.connect(sa)
        except socket.error, msg:
            sock.close()
            continue
    if sock is None:
        print 'Failed to open socket!'
        sys.exit(1)
```

```
        msg = "Hello from ipv6 client"
        print "Send data to server: %s" %msg
        sock.send(msg)
        while True:
            data = sock.recv(BUFSIZE)
            print 'Received from server', repr(data)
            if not data:
                break
        sock.close()
    if __name__ == '__main__':
        parser = argparse.ArgumentParser(description='IPv6 socket client
    example')
        parser.add_argument('--port', action="store", dest="port",
    type=int, required=True)
        given_args = parser.parse_args()
        port = given_args.port
        ipv6_echo_client(port)
```

The server output is as follows:

```
$ python 3_12a_ipv6_echo_server.py --port=8800
Server lisenting on localhost:8800
Connected to ('127.0.0.1', 35034)
Received data from the client: [Hello from ipv6 client]
Sent data echoed back to the client: [Hello from ipv6 client]
```

The client output is as follows:

```
$ python 3_12b_ipv6_echo_client.py --port=8800
Send data to server: Hello from ipv6 client
Received from server 'Hello from ipv6 client'
```

How it works...

The IPv6 echo server first determines its IPv6 information by calling `socket.getaddrinfo()`. Notice that we passed the `AF_UNSPEC` protocol for creating a TCP socket. The resulting information is a tuple of five values. We use three of them, address family, socket type, and protocol, to create a server socket. Then, this socket is bound with the socket address from the previous tuple. It then listens to the incoming connections and accepts them. After a connection is made, it receives data from the client and echoes it back.

On the client-side code, we create an IPv6-compliant client socket instance and send the data using the `send()` method of that instance. When the data is echoed back, the `recv()` method is used to get it back.

4
Programming with HTTP for the Internet

In this chapter, we will cover the following topics:

- Downloading data from an HTTP server
- Serving HTTP requests from your machine
- Extracting cookie information after visiting a website
- Submitting web forms
- Sending web requests through a proxy server
- Checking whether a web page exists with the HEAD request
- Spoofing Mozilla Firefox in your client code
- Saving bandwidth in web requests with the HTTP compression
- Writing an HTTP fail-over client with resume and partial downloading
- Writing a simple HTTPS server code with Python and OpenSSL

Introduction

This chapter explains Python HTTP networking library functions with a few third-party libraries. For example, the `requests` library deals with the HTTP requests in a nicer and cleaner way. The `OpenSSL` library is used in one of the recipes to create a SSL-enabled web server.

Many common HTTP protocol features have been illustrated in a few recipes, for example, the web form submission with `POST`, manipulating header information, use of compression, and so on.

Downloading data from an HTTP server

You would like to write a simple HTTP client to fetch some data from any web server using the native HTTP protocol. This can be the very first steps towards creating your own HTTP browser.

How to do it...

Let us access `www.python.org` with our Pythonic minimal browser that uses Python's `httplib`.

Listing 4.1 explains the following code for a simple HTTP client:

```
#!/usr/bin/env python
# Python Network Programming Cookbook -- Chapter - 4
# This program is optimized for Python 2.7.
# It may run on any other version with/without modifications.


import argparse
import httplib

REMOTE_SERVER_HOST = 'www.python.org'
REMOTE_SERVER_PATH = '/'

class HTTPClient:

  def __init__(self, host):
    self.host = host

  def fetch(self, path):
    http = httplib.HTTP(self.host)

    # Prepare header
    http.putrequest("GET", path)
    http.putheader("User-Agent", __file__)
    http.putheader("Host", self.host)
    http.putheader("Accept", "*/*")
    http.endheaders()

    try:
      errcode, errmsg, headers = http.getreply()

    except Exception, e:
```

```
        print "Client failed error code: %s message:%s headers:%s"
%(errcode, errmsg, headers)
      else:
        print "Got homepage from %s" %self.host

      file = http.getfile()
      return file.read()

if __name__ == "__main__":
  parser = argparse.ArgumentParser(description='HTTP Client
Example')
  parser.add_argument('--host', action="store", dest="host",
default=REMOTE_SERVER_HOST)
  parser.add_argument('--path', action="store", dest="path",
default=REMOTE_SERVER_PATH)
  given_args = parser.parse_args()
  host, path = given_args.host, given_args.path
  client = HTTPClient(host)
  print client.fetch(path)
```

This recipe will by default fetch a page from `www.python.org`. You can run this recipe with or without the host and path arguments. If this script is run, it will show the following output:

```
$  python 4_1_download_data.py --host=www.python.org
Got homepage from www.python.org
<!DOCTYPE html PUBLIC "-//W3C//DTD XHTML 1.0 Transitional//EN" "http://
www.w3.org/TR/xhtml1/DTD/xhtml1-transitional.dtd">
<html xmlns="http://www.w3.og/1999/xhtml" xml:lang="en" lang="en">

<head>
  <meta http-equiv="content-type" content="text/html; charset=utf-8" />
  <title>Python Programming Language &ndash; Official Website</title>
....
```

If you run this recipe with an invalid path, it will show the following server response:

```
$ python 4_1_download_data.py --host='www.python.org' --path='/not-
exist'
Got homepage from www.python.org
<!DOCTYPE html PUBLIC "-//W3C//DTD XHTML 1.0 Transitional//EN" "http://
www.w3.org/TR/xhtml1/DTD/xhtml1-transitional.dtd">
<html xmlns="http://www.w3.org/1999/xhtml" xml:lang="en" lang="en">
<head>
```

```
<meta http-equiv="content-type" content="text/html; charset=utf-8" />
<title>Page Not Found</title>
<meta name="keywords" content="Page Not Found" />
<meta name="description" content="Page Not Found" />
```

How it works...

This recipe defines an `HTTPClient` class that fetches data from the remote host. It is built using Python's native `httplib` library. In the `fetch()` method, it uses the `HTTP()` function and other auxiliary functions to create a dummy HTTP client, such as `putrequest()` or `putheader()`. It first puts the `GET/path` string that is followed by setting up a user agent, which is the name of the current script (`__file__`).

The main request `getreply()` method is put inside a try-except block. The response is retrieved from the `getfile()` method and the stream's content is read.

Serving HTTP requests from your machine

You would like to create your own web server. Your web server should handle client requests and send a simple `hello` message.

How to do it...

Python ships with a very simple web server that can be launched from the command line as follows:

```
$ python -m SimpleHTTPServer 8080
```

This will launch an HTTP web server on port `8080`. You can access this web server from your browser by typing `http://localhost:8080`. This will show the contents of the current directory from where you run the preceding command. If there is any web server index file, for example, `index.html`, inside that directory, your browser will show the contents of `index.html`. However, if you like to have full control over your web server, you need to launch your customized HTTP server..

Listing 4.2 gives the following code for the custom HTTP web server:

```
#!/usr/bin/env python
# Python Network Programming Cookbook -- Chapter - 4
# This program is optimized for Python 2.7.
# It may run on any other version with/without modifications.

import argparse
```

```
import sys
from BaseHTTPServer import BaseHTTPRequestHandler, HTTPServer

DEFAULT_HOST = '127.0.0.1'
DEFAULT_PORT = 8800

class RequestHandler(BaseHTTPRequestHandler):
  """ Custom request handler"""

  def do_GET(self):
    """ Handler for the GET requests """
    self.send_response(200)
    self.send_header('Content-type','text/html')
    self.end_headers()
    # Send the message to browser
    self.wfile.write("Hello from server!")


class CustomHTTPServer(HTTPServer):
  "A custom HTTP server"
  def __init__(self, host, port):
    server_address = (host, port)
    HTTPServer.__init__(self, server_address, RequestHandler)


def run_server(port):
  try:
    server= CustomHTTPServer(DEFAULT_HOST, port)
    print "Custom HTTP server started on port: %s" % port
    server.serve_forever()
  except Exception, err:
    print "Error:%s" %err
  except KeyboardInterrupt:
    print "Server interrupted and is shutting down..."
    server.socket.close()

if __name__ == "__main__":
  parser = argparse.ArgumentParser(description='Simple HTTP Server
Example')
  parser.add_argument('--port', action="store", dest="port",
type=int, default=DEFAULT_PORT)
  given_args = parser.parse_args()
  port = given_args.port
  run_server(port)
```

The following screenshot shows a simple HTTP server:

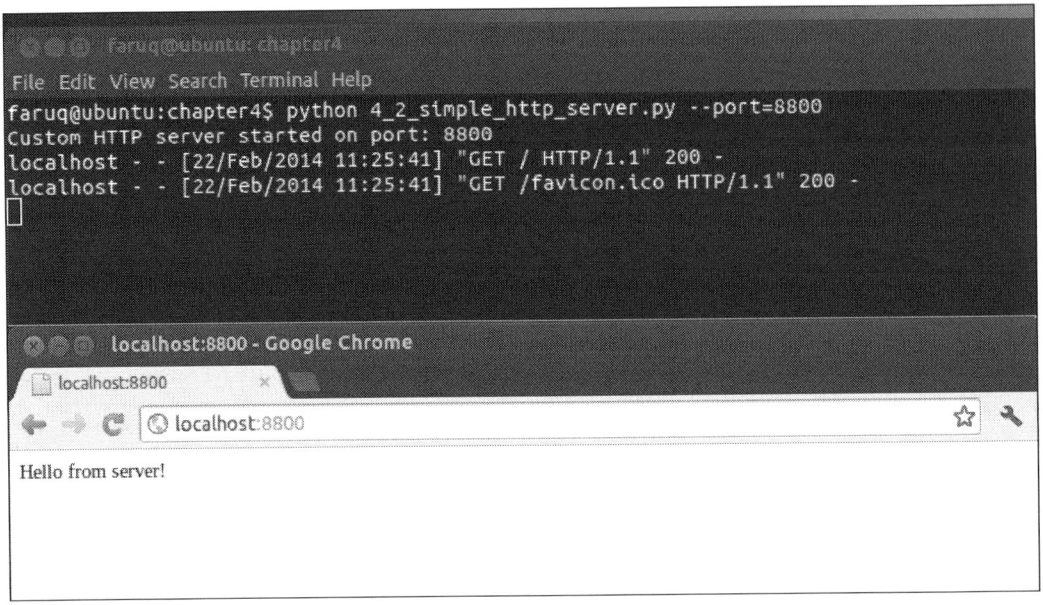

If you run this web server and access the URL from a browser, this will send the one line text `Hello from server!` to the browser, as follows:

```
$ python 4_2_simple_http_server.py --port=8800
Custom HTTP server started on port: 8800
localhost - - [18/Apr/2013 13:39:33] "GET / HTTP/1.1" 200 -
localhost - - [18/Apr/2013 13:39:33] "GET /favicon.ico HTTP/1.1" 200
```

How it works...

In this recipe, we created the `CustomHTTPServer` class inherited from the `HTTPServer` class. In the constructor method, the `CustomHTTPServer` class sets up the server address and port received as a user input. In the constructor, our web server's `RequestHandler` class has been set up. Every time a client is connected, the server handles the request according to this class.

The `RequestHandler` defines the action to handle the client's `GET` request. It sends an HTTP header (code 200) with a success message **Hello from server!** using the `write()` method.

Extracting cookie information after visiting a website

Many websites use cookies to store their various information on to your local disk. You would like to see this cookie information and perhaps log in to that website automatically using cookies.

How to do it...

Let us try to pretend to log in to a popular code-sharing website, `www.bitbucket.org`. We would like to submit the login information on the login page, `https://bitbucket.org/account/signin/?next=/`. The following screenshot shows the login page:

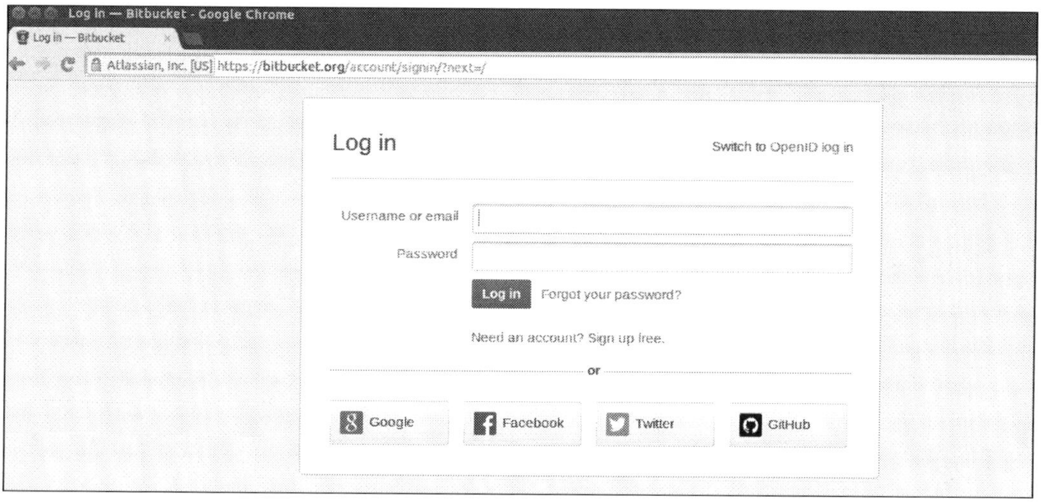

So, we note down the form element IDs and decide which fake values should be submitted. We access this page the first time, and the next time, we access the home page to observe what cookies have been set up.

Listing 4.3 explains extracting cookie information as follows:

```
#!/usr/bin/env python
# Python Network Programming Cookbook -- Chapter - 4
# This program is optimized for Python 2.7.
# It may run on any other version with/without modifications.

import cookielib
import urllib
import urllib2

ID_USERNAME = 'id_username'
```

```
ID_PASSWORD = 'id_password'
USERNAME = 'you@email.com'
PASSWORD = 'mypassword'
LOGIN_URL = 'https://bitbucket.org/account/signin/?next=/'
NORMAL_URL = 'https://bitbucket.org/'

def extract_cookie_info():
  """ Fake login to a site with cookie"""
  # setup cookie jar
  cj = cookielib.CookieJar()
  login_data = urllib.urlencode({ID_USERNAME : USERNAME,
  ID_PASSWORD : PASSWORD})
  # create url opener
  opener = urllib2.build_opener(urllib2.HTTPCookieProcessor(cj))
  resp = opener.open(LOGIN_URL, login_data)

  # send login info
  for cookie in cj:
    print "----First time cookie: %s --> %s" %(cookie.name,
cookie.value)
    print "Headers: %s" %resp.headers

  # now access without any login info
  resp = opener.open(NORMAL_URL)
  for cookie in cj:
    print "++++Second time cookie: %s --> %s" %(cookie.name,
cookie.value)

  print "Headers: %s" %resp.headers

if __name__ == '__main__':
  extract_cookie_info()
```

Running this recipe results in the following output:

```
$ python 4_3_extract_cookie_information.py
----First time cookie: bb_session --> aed58dde1228571bf60466581790566d
Headers: Server: nginx/1.2.4
Date: Sun, 05 May 2013 15:13:56 GMT
Content-Type: text/html; charset=utf-8
Content-Length: 21167
Connection: close
X-Served-By: bitbucket04
Content-Language: en
X-Static-Version: c67fb01467cf
```

```
Expires: Sun, 05 May 2013 15:13:56 GMT
Vary: Accept-Language, Cookie
Last-Modified: Sun, 05 May 2013 15:13:56 GMT
X-Version: 14f9c66ad9db
ETag: "3ba81d9eb350c295a453b5ab6e88935e"
X-Request-Count: 310
Cache-Control: max-age=0
Set-Cookie: bb_session=aed58dde1228571bf60466581790566d; expires=Sun, 19-
May-2013 15:13:56 GMT; httponly; Max-Age=1209600; Path=/; secure

Strict-Transport-Security: max-age=2592000
X-Content-Type-Options: nosniff

++++Second time cookie: bb_session --> aed58dde1228571bf60466581790566d
Headers: Server: nginx/1.2.4
Date: Sun, 05 May 2013 15:13:57 GMT
Content-Type: text/html; charset=utf-8
Content-Length: 36787
Connection: close
X-Served-By: bitbucket02
Content-Language: en
X-Static-Version: c67fb01467cf
Vary: Accept-Language, Cookie
X-Version: 14f9c66ad9db
X-Request-Count: 97
Strict-Transport-Security: max-age=2592000
X-Content-Type-Options: nosniff
```

How it works...

We have used Python's `cookielib` and set up a cookie jar, `cj`. The login data has been encoded using `urllib.urlencode`. `urllib2` has a `build_opener()` method, which takes the predefined cookie jar with an instance of `HTTPCookieProcessor()` and returns a URL opener. We call this opener twice: once for the login page and once for the home page of the website. It seems that only one cookie, `bb_session`, was set with the set-cookie directive present in the page header. More information about `cookielib` can be found on the official Python documentation site at `http://docs.python.org/2/library/cookielib.html`.

Submitting web forms

During web browsing, we submit web forms many times in a day. Now, you would like do that using the Python code.

Getting ready

This recipe uses a third-party Python module called `requests`. You can install the compatible version of this module by following the instructions from `http://docs.python-requests.org/en/latest/user/install/`. For example, you can use `pip` to install `requests` from the command line as follows:

```
$ pip install requests
```

How to do it...

Let us submit some fake data to register with `www.twitter.com`. Each form submission has two methods: `GET` and `POST`. The less sensitive data, for example, search queries, are usually submitted by `GET` and the more sensitive data is sent via the `POST` method. Let us try submitting data with both of them.

Listing 4.4 explains the submit web forms, as follows:

```
#!/usr/bin/env python
# Python Network Programming Cookbook -- Chapter - 4
# This program is optimized for Python 2.7.
# It may run on any other version with/without modifications.

import requests
import urllib
import urllib2

ID_USERNAME = 'signup-user-name'
ID_EMAIL = 'signup-user-email'
ID_PASSWORD = 'signup-user-password'
USERNAME = 'username'
EMAIL = 'you@email.com'
PASSWORD = 'yourpassword'
SIGNUP_URL = 'https://twitter.com/account/create'


def submit_form():
    """Submit a form"""
    payload = {ID_USERNAME : USERNAME,
```

```
                ID_EMAIL    :  EMAIL,
                ID_PASSWORD : PASSWORD,}

        # make a get request
        resp = requests.get(SIGNUP_URL)
        print "Response to GET request: %s" %resp.content

        # send POST request
        resp = requests.post(SIGNUP_URL, payload)
        print "Headers from a POST request response: %s" %resp.headers
        #print "HTML Response: %s" %resp.read()

    if __name__ == '__main__':
        submit_form()
```

If you run this script, you will see the following output:

```
$ python 4_4_submit_web_form.py
Response to GET request: <?xml version="1.0" encoding="UTF-8"?>
<hash>
  <error>This method requires a POST.</error>
  <request>/account/create</request>
</hash>

Headers from a POST request response: {'status': '200 OK', 'content-
length': '21064', 'set-cookie': '_twitter_sess=BAh7CD--
d2865d40d1365eeb2175559dc5e6b99f64ea39ff; domain=.twitter.com;
path=/; HttpOnly', 'expires': 'Tue, 31 Mar 1981 05:00:00 GMT',
'vary': 'Accept-Encoding', 'last-modified': 'Sun, 05 May 2013
15:59:27 GMT', 'pragma': 'no-cache', 'date': 'Sun, 05 May 2013
15:59:27 GMT', 'x-xss-protection': '1; mode=block', 'x-transaction':
'a4b425eda23b5312', 'content-encoding': 'gzip', 'strict-transport-
security': 'max-age=631138519', 'server': 'tfe', 'x-mid':
'f7cde9a3f3d111310427116adc90bf3e8c95e868', 'x-runtime': '0.09969',
'etag': '"7af6f92a7f7b4d37a6454caa6094071d"', 'cache-control': 'no-
cache, no-store, must-revalidate, pre-check=0, post-check=0', 'x-
frame-options': 'SAMEORIGIN', 'content-type': 'text/html;
charset=utf-8'}
```

How it works...

This recipe uses a third-party module, `requests`. It has convenient wrapper methods, `get()` and `post()`, that do the URL encoding of data and submit forms properly.

In this recipe, we created a data payload with a username, password, and e-mail for creating the Twitter account. When we first submit the form with the `GET` method, the Twitter website returns an error saying that the page only supports `POST`. After we submit the data with `POST`, the page processes it. We can confirm this from the header data.

Sending web requests through a proxy server

You would like to browse web pages through a proxy. If you have configured your browser with a proxy server and that works, you can try this recipe. Otherwise, you can use any of the public proxy servers available on the Internet.

Getting ready

You need to have access to a proxy server. You can find a free proxy server by searching on Google or on any other search engine. Here, for the sake of demonstration, we have used `165.24.10.8`.

How to do it...

Let us send our HTTP request through a public domain proxy server.

Listing 4.5 explains proxying web requests across a proxy server as follows:

```
#!/usr/bin/env python
# Python Network Programming Cookbook -- Chapter - 4
# This program is optimized for Python 2.7.
# It may run on any other version with/without modifications.

import urllib

URL = 'https://www.github.com'
PROXY_ADDRESS = "165.24.10.8:8080"

if __name__ == '__main__':
  resp = urllib.urlopen(URL, proxies = {"http" : PROXY_ADDRESS})
  print "Proxy server returns response headers: %s "
%resp.headers
```

If you run this script, it will show the following output:

```
$ python 4_5_proxy_web_request.py
Proxy server returns response headers: Server: GitHub.com
Date: Sun, 05 May 2013 16:16:04 GMT
Content-Type: text/html; charset=utf-8
Connection: close
Status: 200 OK
Cache-Control: private, max-age=0, must-revalidate
Strict-Transport-Security: max-age=2592000
X-Frame-Options: deny
Set-Cookie: logged_in=no; domain=.github.com; path=/; expires=Thu, 05-
May-2033 16:16:04 GMT; HttpOnly
Set-Cookie: _gh_sess=BAh7...; path=/; expires=Sun, 01-Jan-2023 00:00:00
GMT; secure; HttpOnly
X-Runtime: 8
ETag: "66fcc37865eb05c19b2d15fbb44cd7a9"
Content-Length: 10643
Vary: Accept-Encoding
```

How it works...

This is a short recipe where we access the social code-sharing site, `www.github.com`, with a public proxy server found on Google search. The proxy address argument has been passed to the `urlopen()` method of `urllib`. We print the HTTP header of response to show that the proxy settings work here.

Checking whether a web page exists with the HEAD request

You would like to check the existence of a web page without downloading the HTML content. This means that we need to send a `get HEAD` request with a browser client. According to Wikipedia, the `HEAD` request asks for the response identical to the one that would correspond to a `GET` request, but without the response body. This is useful for retrieving meta-information written in response headers, without having to transport the entire content.

How to do it...

We would like to send a `HEAD` request to `www.python.org`. This will not download the content of the homepage, rather it checks whether the server returns one of the valid responses, for example, `OK`, `FOUND`, `MOVED PERMANENTLY`, and so on.

Listing 4.6 explains checking a web page with the HEAD request as follows:

```
#!/usr/bin/env python
# Python Network Programming Cookbook -- Chapter - 4
# This program is optimized for Python 2.7.
# It may run on any other version with/without modifications.
import argparse
import httplib
import urlparse
import re
import urllib

DEFAULT_URL = 'http://www.python.org'
HTTP_GOOD_CODES =  [httplib.OK, httplib.FOUND, httplib.MOVED_
PERMANENTLY]

def get_server_status_code(url):
  """
  Download just the header of a URL and
  return the server's status code.
  """
  host, path = urlparse.urlparse(url)[1:3]
  try:
    conn = httplib.HTTPConnection(host)
    conn.request('HEAD', path)
    return conn.getresponse().status
    except StandardError:
  return None

if __name__ == '__main__':
  parser = argparse.ArgumentParser(description='Example HEAD 
Request')
  parser.add_argument('--url', action="store", dest="url", 
default=DEFAULT_URL)
  given_args = parser.parse_args()
  url = given_args.url
  if get_server_status_code(url) in HTTP_GOOD_CODES:
    print "Server: %s status is OK: " %url
  else:
    print "Server: %s status is NOT OK!" %url
```

Running this script shows the success or error if the page is found by the HEAD request as follows:

```
$ python 4_6_checking_webpage_with_HEAD_request.py
Server: http://www.python.org status is OK!
$ python 4_6_checking_webpage_with_HEAD_request.py --url=http://www.
zytho.org
Server: http://www.zytho.org status is NOT OK!
```

How it works...

We used the `HTTPConnection()` method of `httplib`, which can make a `HEAD` request to a server. We can specify the path if necessary. Here, the `HTTPConnection()` method checks the home page or path of `www.python.org`. However, if the URL is not correct, it can't find the return response inside the accepted list of return codes.

Spoofing Mozilla Firefox in your client code

From your Python code, you would like to pretend to the web server that you are browsing from Mozilla Firefox.

How to do it...

You can send the custom user-agent values in the HTTP request header.

Listing 4.7 explains spoofing Mozilla Firefox in your client code as follows:

```
#!/usr/bin/env python
# Python Network Programming Cookbook -- Chapter - 4
# This program is optimized for Python 2.7.
# It may run on any other version with/without modifications.

import urllib2

BROWSER = 'Mozilla/5.0 (Windows NT 5.1; rv:20.0) Gecko/20100101
Firefox/20.0'
URL = 'http://www.python.org'

def spoof_firefox():
  opener = urllib2.build_opener()
  opener.addheaders = [('User-agent', BROWSER)]
  result = opener.open(URL)
  print "Response headers:"
  for header in  result.headers.headers:
    print "\t",header

if __name__ == '__main__':
  spoof_firefox()
```

If you run this script, you will see the following output:

```
$ python 4_7_spoof_mozilla_firefox_in_client_code.py
Response headers:
    Date: Sun, 05 May 2013 16:56:36 GMT
    Server: Apache/2.2.16 (Debian)
```

```
Last-Modified: Sun, 05 May 2013 00:51:40 GMT
ETag: "105800d-5280-4dbedfcb07f00"
Accept-Ranges: bytes
Content-Length: 21120
Vary: Accept-Encoding
Connection: close
Content-Type: text/html
```

How it works...

We used the `build_opener()` method of `urllib2` to create our custom browser whose user-agent string has been set up as `Mozilla/5.0 (Windows NT 5.1; rv:20.0) Gecko/20100101 Firefox/20.0`.

Saving bandwidth in web requests with the HTTP compression

You would like to give your web server users better performance in downloading web pages. By compressing HTTP data, you can speed up the serving of web contents.

How to do it...

Let us create a web server that serves contents after compressing it to the `gzip` format.

Listing 4.8 explains the HTTP compression as follows:

```
#!/usr/bin/env python
# Python Network Programming Cookbook -- Chapter - 4
# This program is optimized for Python 2.7.
# It may run on any other version with/without modifications.
import argparse
import string
import os
import sys
import gzip
import cStringIO
from BaseHTTPServer import BaseHTTPRequestHandler, HTTPServer

DEFAULT_HOST = '127.0.0.1'
DEFAULT_PORT = 8800
HTML_CONTENT = """<html><body><h1>Compressed Hello  World!</h1></
body></html>"""
```

```
class RequestHandler(BaseHTTPRequestHandler):
  """ Custom request handler"""

  def do_GET(self):
    """ Handler for the GET requests """
    self.send_response(200)
    self.send_header('Content-type','text/html')
    self.send_header('Content-Encoding','gzip')

    zbuf = self.compress_buffer(HTML_CONTENT)
    sys.stdout.write("Content-Encoding: gzip\r\n")
    self.send_header('Content-Length',len(zbuf))
    self.end_headers()

  # Send the message to browser
    zbuf = self.compress_buffer(HTML_CONTENT)
    sys.stdout.write("Content-Encoding: gzip\r\n")
    sys.stdout.write("Content-Length: %d\r\n" % (len(zbuf)))
    sys.stdout.write("\r\n")
    self.wfile.write(zbuf)
  return

  def compress_buffer(self, buf):
    zbuf = cStringIO.StringIO()
    zfile = gzip.GzipFile(mode = 'wb',  fileobj = zbuf, 
compresslevel = 6)
    zfile.write(buf)
    zfile.close()
    return zbuf.getvalue()


if __name__ == '__main__':
  parser = argparse.ArgumentParser(description='Simple HTTP Server 
Example')
  parser.add_argument('--port', action="store", dest="port", 
type=int, default=DEFAULT_PORT)
  given_args = parser.parse_args()
  port = given_args.port
  server_address =  (DEFAULT_HOST, port)
  server = HTTPServer(server_address, RequestHandler)
  server.serve_forever()
```

You can run this script and see the `Compressed Hello World!` text (as a result of the HTTP compression) on your browser screen when accessing `http://localhost:8800` as follows:

```
$ python 4_8_http_compression.py
localhost - - [22/Feb/2014 12:01:26] "GET / HTTP/1.1" 200 -
Content-Encoding: gzip
Content-Encoding: gzip
Content-Length: 71
localhost - - [22/Feb/2014 12:01:26] "GET /favicon.ico HTTP/1.1" 200 -
Content-Encoding: gzip
Content-Encoding: gzip
Content-Length: 71
```

The following screenshot illustrates serving compressed content by a web server:

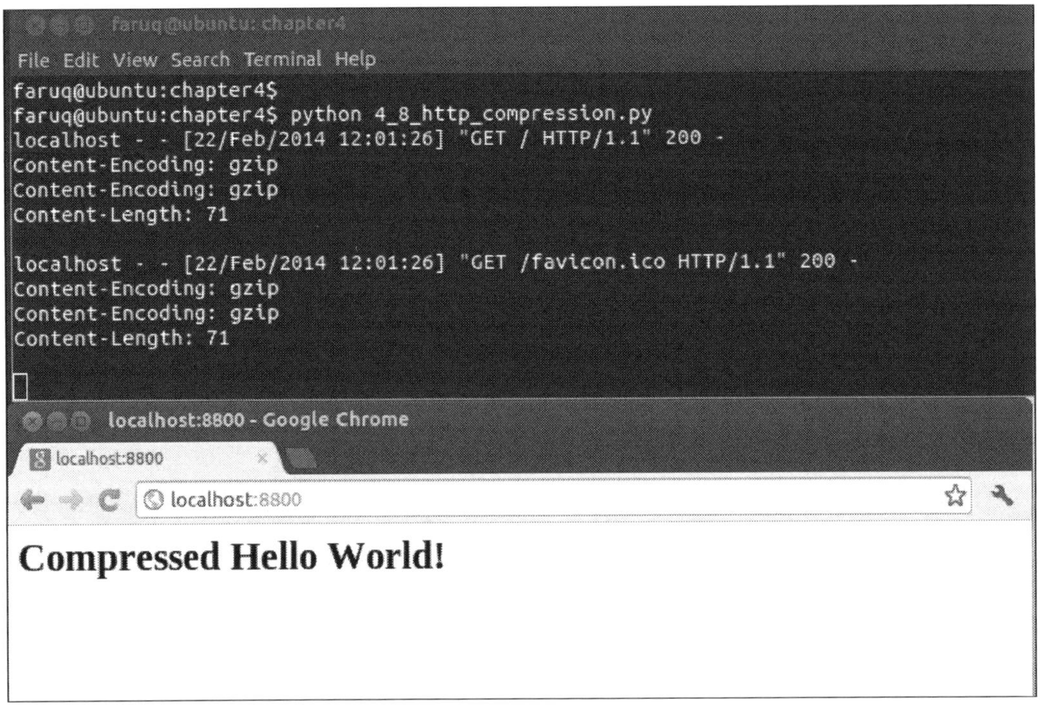

How it works...

We created a web server by instantiating the `HTTPServer` class from the `BaseHTTPServer` module. We attached a custom request handler to this server instance, which compresses every client response using a `compress_buffer()` method. A predefined HTML content has been supplied to the clients.

Writing an HTTP fail-over client with resume and partial downloading

You would like to create a fail-over client that will resume downloading a file if it fails for any reason in the first instance.

How to do it...

Let us download the Python 2.7 code from `www.python.org`. A `resume_download()` file will resume any unfinished download of that file.

Listing 4.9 explains resume downloading as follows:

```
#!/usr/bin/env python
# Python Network Programming Cookbook -- Chapter - 4
# This program is optimized for Python 2.7.# It may run on any other
version with/without modifications.

import urllib, os
TARGET_URL = 'http://python.org/ftp/python/2.7.4/'
TARGET_FILE = 'Python-2.7.4.tgz'

class CustomURLOpener(urllib.FancyURLopener):
  """Override FancyURLopener to skip error 206 (when a
    partial file is being sent)
  """
  def http_error_206(self, url, fp, errcode, errmsg, headers,
data=None):
    pass

  def resume_download():
    file_exists = False
    CustomURLClass = CustomURLOpener()
  if os.path.exists(TARGET_FILE):
    out_file = open(TARGET_FILE,"ab")
    file_exists = os.path.getsize(TARGET_FILE)
    #If the file exists, then only download the unfinished part
    CustomURLClass.addheader("Download range","bytes=%s-" %
(file_exists))
  else:
    out_file = open(TARGET_FILE,"wb")

  web_page = CustomURLClass.open(TARGET_URL + TARGET_FILE)

  #If the file exists, but we already have the whole thing, don't
```

```
download again
    if int(web_page.headers['Content-Length']) == file_exists:
      loop = 0
      print "File already downloaded!"

    byte_count = 0
    while True:
      data = web_page.read(8192)
      if not data:
        break
      out_file.write(data)
      byte_count = byte_count + len(data)

    web_page.close()
    out_file.close()

    for k,v in web_page.headers.items():
      print k, "=",v
    print "File copied", byte_count, "bytes from", web_page.url

  if __name__ == '__main__':
    resume_download()
```

Running this script will result in the following output:

```
$   python 4_9_http_fail_over_client.py
content-length = 14489063
content-encoding = x-gzip
accept-ranges = bytes
connection = close
server = Apache/2.2.16 (Debian)
last-modified = Sat, 06 Apr 2013 14:16:10 GMT
content-range = bytes 0-14489062/14489063
etag = "1748016-dd15e7-4d9b1d8685e80"
date = Tue, 07 May 2013 12:51:31 GMT
content-type = application/x-tar
File copied 14489063 bytes from http://python.org/ftp/python/2.7.4/
Python-2.7.4.tgz
```

How it works...

In this recipe, we created a custom URL opener class inheriting from the `FancyURLopener` method of `urllib`, but `http_error_206()` is overridden where partial content is downloaded. So, our method checks the existence of the target file and if it is not present, it tries to download with the custom URL opener class.

Writing a simple HTTPS server code with Python and OpenSSL

You need a secure web server code written in Python. You already have your SSL keys and certificate files ready with you.

Getting ready

You need to install the third-party Python module, `pyOpenSSL`. This can be grabbed from PyPI (`https://pypi.python.org/pypi/pyOpenSSL`). Both on Windows and Linux hosts, you may need to install some additional packages, which are documented at `http://pythonhosted.org//pyOpenSSL/`.

How to do it...

After placing a certificate file on the current working folder, we can create a web server that makes use of this certificate to serve encrypted content to the clients.

Listing 4.10 explains the code for a secure HTTP server as follows:

```
#!/usr/bin/env python
# Python Network Programming Cookbook -- Chapter - 4
# This program is optimized for Python 2.7.
# It may run on any other version with/without modifications.
# Requires pyOpenSSL and SSL packages installed

import socket, os
from SocketServer import BaseServer
from BaseHTTPServer import HTTPServer
from SimpleHTTPServer import SimpleHTTPRequestHandler
from OpenSSL import SSL

class SecureHTTPServer(HTTPServer):
  def __init__(self, server_address, HandlerClass):
    BaseServer.__init__(self, server_address, HandlerClass)
    ctx = SSL.Context(SSL.SSLv23_METHOD)
    fpem = 'server.pem' # location of the server private key and
the server certificate
    ctx.use_privatekey_file (fpem)
    ctx.use_certificate_file(fpem)
    self.socket = SSL.Connection(ctx,
socket.socket(self.address_family, self.socket_type))
    self.server_bind()
    self.server_activate()
```

```
class SecureHTTPRequestHandler(SimpleHTTPRequestHandler):
  def setup(self):
    self.connection = self.request
    self.rfile = socket._fileobject(self.request, "rb",
self.rbufsize)
    self.wfile = socket._fileobject(self.request, "wb",
self.wbufsize)


  def run_server(HandlerClass = SecureHTTPRequestHandler,
    ServerClass = SecureHTTPServer):
    server_address = ('', 4443) # port needs to be accessible by
user
    server = ServerClass(server_address, HandlerClass)
    running_address = server.socket.getsockname()
    print "Serving HTTPS Server on %s:%s ..."
%(running_address[0], running_address[1])
    server.serve_forever()

if __name__ == '__main__':
  run_server()
```

If you run this script, it will result in the following output:

```
$ python 4_10_https_server.py
Serving HTTPS Server on 0.0.0.0:4443 ...
```

How it works...

If you notice the previous recipes that create the web server, there is not much difference in terms of the basic procedure. The main difference is in applying the SSL `Context()` method with the `SSLv23_METHOD` argument. We have created the SSL socket with the Python OpenSSL third-party module's `Connection()` class. This class takes this context object along with the address family and socket type.

The server's certificate file is kept in the current directory, and this has been applied with the context object. Finally, the server has been activated with the `server_activate()` method.

5

E-mail Protocols, FTP, and CGI Programming

In this chapter, we will cover the following recipes:

- Listing the files in a remote FTP server
- Uploading a local file to a remote FTP server
- E-mailing your current working directory as a compressed ZIP file
- Downloading your Google e-mail with POP3
- Checking your remote e-mail with IMAP
- Sending an e-mail with an attachment via the Gmail SMTP server
- Writing a guestbook for your (Python-based) web server with CGI

Introduction

This chapter explores the FTP, e-mail, and CGI communications protocol with a Python recipe. Python is a very efficient and friendly language. Using Python, you can easily code simple FTP actions such as a file download and upload.

There are some interesting recipes in this chapter, such as manipulating your Google e-mail, also known as the Gmail account, from your Python script. You can use these recipes to check, download, and send e-mails with IMAP, POP3, and SMTP protocols. In another recipe, a web server with CGI also demonstrates the basic CGI action, such as writing a guest comment form in your web application.

Listing the files in a remote FTP server

You would like to list the files available on the official Linux kernel's FTP site, `ftp.kernel.org`. You can select any other FTP site to try this recipe.

Getting ready

If you work on a real FTP site with a user account, you need a username and password. However, in this instance, you don't need a username (and password) with Linux kernel's FTP site as you can log in anonymously.

How to do it...

We can use the `ftplib` library to fetch files from our selected FTP site. A detailed documentation of this library can be found at `http://docs.python.org/2/library/ftplib.html`.

Let us see how we can fetch some files with `ftplib`.

Listing 5.1 gives a simple FTP connection test as follows:

```
#!/usr/bin/env python
# Python Network Programming Cookbook -- Chapter - 5
# This program is optimized for Python 2.7.
# It may run on any other version with/without modifications.

FTP_SERVER_URL = 'ftp.kernel.org'

import ftplib
def test_ftp_connection(path, username, email):
    #Open ftp connection
    ftp = ftplib.FTP(path, username, email)

   #List the files in the /pub directory
    ftp.cwd("/pub")
    print "File list at %s:" %path
    files = ftp.dir()
    print files

    ftp.quit()
if __name__ == '__main__':
    test_ftp_connection(path=FTP_SERVER_URL, username='anonymous',
                        email='nobody@nourl.com',
                        )
```

This recipe will list the files and folders present in the FTP path, `ftp.kernel.org/pub`. If you run this script, you can see the following output:

```
$ python 5_1_list_files_on_ftp_server.py
File list at ftp.kernel.org:
drwxrwxr-x    6 ftp      ftp          4096 Dec 01  2011 dist
drwxr-xr-x   13 ftp      ftp          4096 Nov 16  2011 linux
drwxrwxr-x    3 ftp      ftp          4096 Sep 23  2008 media
drwxr-xr-x   17 ftp      ftp          4096 Jun 06  2012 scm
drwxrwxr-x    2 ftp      ftp          4096 Dec 01  2011 site
drwxr-xr-x   13 ftp      ftp          4096 Nov 27  2011 software
drwxr-xr-x    3 ftp      ftp          4096 Apr 30  2008 tools
```

How it works...

This recipe uses `ftplib` to create an FTP client session with `ftp.kernel.org`. The `test_ftp_connection()` function takes the FTP path, username, and e-mail address for connecting to the FTP server.

An FTP client session can be created by calling the `FTP()` function of `ftplib` with the preceding connection's credentials. This returns a client handle which then can be used to run the usual ftp commands, such as the command to change the working directory or `cwd()`. The `dir()` method returns the directory listing.

It is good idea to quit the FTP session by calling `ftp.quit()`.

Uploading a local file to a remote FTP server

You would like to upload a file to an FTP server.

Getting ready

Let us set up a local FTP server. In Unix/Linux, you can install the **wu-ftpd** package using the following command:

```
$ sudo apt-get install wu-ftpd
```

On a Windows machine, you can install the FileZilla FTP server, which can be downloaded from `https://filezilla-project.org/download.php?type=server`.

You should create an FTP user account following the FTP server package's user manual.

You would also like to upload a file to an ftp server. You can specify the server address, login credentials, and filename as the input argument of your script. You should create a local file called `readme.txt` with any text in it.

How to do it...

Using the following script, let's set up a local FTP server. In Unix/Linux, you can install the wu-ftpd package. Then, you can upload a file to the logged-in user's home directory. You can specify the server address, login credentials, and filename as the input argument of your script.

Listing 5.2 gives the FTP Upload Example as follows:

```
#!/usr/bin/env python
# Python Network Programming Cookbook -- Chapter - 5
# This program is optimized for Python 2.7.
# It may run on any other version with/without modifications.

import os
import argparse
import ftplib

import getpass
LOCAL_FTP_SERVER = 'localhost'
LOCAL_FILE = 'readme.txt'
def ftp_upload(ftp_server, username, password, file_name):
    print "Connecting to FTP server: %s" %ftp_server
    ftp = ftplib.FTP(ftp_server)
    print "Login to FTP server: user=%s" %username
    ftp.login(username, password)
    ext = os.path.splitext(file_name)[1]
    if ext in (".txt", ".htm", ".html"):
        ftp.storlines("STOR " + file_name, open(file_name))
    else:
        ftp.storbinary("STOR " + file_name, open(file_name, "rb"),
1024)
    print "Uploaded file: %s" %file_name

if __name__ == '__main__':
    parser = argparse.ArgumentParser(description='FTP Server Upload
Example')
    parser.add_argument('--ftp-server', action="store", dest="ftp_
server", default=LOCAL_FTP_SERVER)
    parser.add_argument('--file-name', action="store", dest="file_
name", default=LOCAL_FILE)
    parser.add_argument('--username', action="store", dest="username",
default=getpass.getuser())
    given_args = parser.parse_args()
    ftp_server, file_name, username = given_args.ftp_server, given_
args.file_name, given_args.username
    password = getpass.getpass(prompt="Enter you FTP password: ")
    ftp_upload(ftp_server, username, password, file_name)
```

If you set up a local FTP server and run the following script, this script will log in to the FTP server and then will upload a file. If a filename argument is not supplied from command line by default, it will upload the `readme.txt` file.

```
$ python 5_2_upload_file_to_ftp_server.py
Enter your FTP password:
Connecting to FTP server: localhost
Login to FTP server: user=faruq
Uploaded file: readme.txt

$ cat /home/faruq/readme.txt
This file describes what to do with the .bz2 files you see elsewhere
on this site (ftp.kernel.org).
```

How it works...

In this recipe, we assume that a local FTP server is running. Alternatively, you can connect to a remote FTP server. The `ftp_upload()` method uses the `FTP()`function of Python's `ftplib` to create an FTP connection object. With the `login()` method, it logs in to the server.

After a successful login, the `ftp` object sends the STOR command with either the `storlines()` or `storbinary()` method. The first method is used for sending ASCII text files such as HTML or text files. The latter method is used for binary data such as zipped archive.

It's a good idea to wrap these FTP methods with `try-catch` error-handling blocks, which is not shown here for the sake of brevity.

E-mailing your current working directory as a compressed ZIP file

It might be interesting to send the current working directory contents as a compressed ZIP archive. You can use this recipe to quickly share your files with your friends.

Getting ready

If you don't have any mail server installed on your machine, you need to install a local mail server such as `postfix`. On a Debian/Ubuntu system, this can be installed with default settings using `apt-get`, as shown in the following command:

```
$ sudo apt-get install postfix
```

How to do it...

Let us first compress the current directory and then create an e-mail message. We can send the e-mail message via an external SMTP host, or we can use a local e-mail server to do this. Like other recipes, let us get the sender and recipient information from parsing the command-line inputs.

Listing 5.3 shows how to convert an e-mail folder into a compressed ZIP file as follows:

```
#!/usr/bin/env python
# Python Network Programming Cookbook -- Chapter - 5
# This program is optimized for Python 2.7.
# It may run on any other version with/without modifications.

import os
import argparse
import smtplib
import zipfile
import tempfile
from email import encoders
from email.mime.base import MIMEBase
from email.mime.multipart import MIMEMultipart
def email_dir_zipped(sender, recipient):
    zf = tempfile.TemporaryFile(prefix='mail', suffix='.zip')
    zip = zipfile.ZipFile(zf, 'w')
    print "Zipping current dir: %s" %os.getcwd()
    for file_name in os.listdir(os.getcwd()):
        zip.write(file_name)
    zip.close()
    zf.seek(0)
    # Create the message
    print "Creating email message..."
    email_msg = MIMEMultipart()
    email_msg['Subject'] = 'File from path %s' %os.getcwd()
    email_msg['To'] = ', '.join(recipient)
    email_msg['From'] = sender
    email_msg.preamble = 'Testing email from Python.\n'
    msg = MIMEBase('application', 'zip')
    msg.set_payload(zf.read())
    encoders.encode_base64(msg)
    msg.add_header('Content-Disposition', 'attachment',
                   filename=os.getcwd()[-1] + '.zip')
    email_msg.attach(msg)
    email_msg = email_msg.as_string()
```

```
        # send the message
        print "Sending email message..."
        smtp = None
        try:
            smtp = smtplib.SMTP('localhost')
            smtp.set_debuglevel(1)
            smtp.sendmail(sender, recipient, email_msg)
        except Exception, e:
            print "Error: %s" %str(e)
        finally:
            if smtp:
               smtp.close()

if __name__ == '__main__':
    parser = argparse.ArgumentParser(description='Email Example')
    parser.add_argument('--sender', action="store", dest="sender",
default='you@you.com')
    parser.add_argument('--recipient', action="store",
dest="recipient")
    given_args = parser.parse_args()
    email_dir_zipped(given_args.sender, given_args.recipient)
```

Running this recipe shows the following output. The extra output is shown because we enabled the e-mail debug level.

```
$ python 5_3_email_current_dir_zipped.py --recipient=faruq@localhost
Zipping current dir: /home/faruq/Dropbox/PacktPub/pynet-cookbook/
pynetcookbook_code/chapter5
Creating email message...
Sending email message...
send: 'ehlo [127.0.0.1]\r\n'
reply: '250-debian6.debian2013.com\r\n'
reply: '250-PIPELINING\r\n'
reply: '250-SIZE 10240000\r\n'
reply: '250-VRFY\r\n'
reply: '250-ETRN\r\n'
reply: '250-STARTTLS\r\n'
reply: '250-ENHANCEDSTATUSCODES\r\n'
reply: '250-8BITMIME\r\n'
reply: '250 DSN\r\n'
reply: retcode (250); Msg: debian6.debian2013.com
PIPELINING
```

```
SIZE 10240000
VRFY
ETRN
STARTTLS
ENHANCEDSTATUSCODES
8BITMIME
DSN
send: 'mail FROM:<you@you.com> size=9141\r\n'
reply: '250 2.1.0 Ok\r\n'
reply: retcode (250); Msg: 2.1.0 Ok
send: 'rcpt TO:<faruq@localhost>\r\n'
reply: '250 2.1.5 Ok\r\n'
reply: retcode (250); Msg: 2.1.5 Ok
send: 'data\r\n'
reply: '354 End data with <CR><LF>.<CR><LF>\r\n'
reply: retcode (354); Msg: End data with <CR><LF>.<CR><LF>
data: (354, 'End data with <CR><LF>.<CR><LF>')
send: 'Content-Type: multipart/mixed;
boundary="===============0388489101==...[TRUNCATED]
reply: '250 2.0.0 Ok: queued as 42D2F34A996\r\n'
reply: retcode (250); Msg: 2.0.0 Ok: queued as 42D2F34A996
data: (250, '2.0.0 Ok: queued as 42D2F34A996')
```

How it works...

We have used Python's `zipfile`, `smtplib` and an `email` module to achieve our objective of e-mailing a folder as a zipped archive. This is done using the `email_dir_zipped()` method. This method takes two arguments: the sender and recipient's e-mail addresses to create the e-mail message.

In order to create a ZIP archive, we create a temporary file with the `tempfile` module's `TemporaryFile()` class. We supply a filename prefix, `mail`, and suffix, `.zip`. Then, we initialize the ZIP archive object with the `ZipFile()` class by passing the temporary file as its argument. Later, we add files of the current directory with the ZIP object's `write()` method call.

To send an e-mail, we create a multipart MIME message with the `MIMEmultipart()` class from the `email.mime.multipart` module. Like our usual e-mail message, the subject, recipient, and sender information is added in the e-mail header.

We create the e-mail attachment with the `MIMEBase()` method. Here, we first specify the application/ZIP header and call `set_payload()` on this message object. Then, in order to encode the message correctly, the `encode_base64()` method from encoder's module is used. It is also helpful to use the `add_header()` method to construct the attachment header. Now, our attachment is ready to be included in the main e-mail message with an `attach()` method call.

Sending an e-mail requires you to call the `SMTP()` class instance of `smtplib`. There is a `sendmail()` method that will utilize the routine provided by the OS to actually send the e-mail message correctly. Its details are hidden under the hood. However, you can see a detailed interaction by enabling the debug option as shown in this recipe.

See also

- Further information about the Python libraries can be found at the URL `http://docs.python.org/2/library/smtplib.html`

Downloading your Google e-mail with POP3

You would like to download your Google (or virtually any other e-mail provider's) e-mail via the POP3 protocol.

Getting ready

To run this recipe, you should have an e-mail account with Google or any other service provider.

How to do it...

Here, we attempt to download the first e-mail message from a user's Google e-mail account. The username is supplied from a command line, but the password is kept secret and not passed from the command line. This is rather entered while the script is running and kept hidden from display.

Listing 5.4 shows how to download our Google e-mail via `POP3` as follows:

```
#!/usr/bin/env python
# Python Network Programming Cookbook -- Chapter - 5
# This program is optimized for Python 2.7.
# It may run on any other version with/without modifications.

import argparse
import getpass
import poplib
GOOGLE_POP3_SERVER = 'pop.googlemail.com'
```

```
def download_email(username):
    mailbox = poplib.POP3_SSL(GOOGLE_POP3_SERVER, '995')
    mailbox.user(username)
    password = getpass.getpass(prompt="Enter you Google password: ")
    mailbox.pass_(password)
    num_messages = len(mailbox.list()[1])
    print "Total emails: %s" %num_messages
    print "Getting last message"
    for msg in mailbox.retr(num_messages)[1]:
        print msg
    mailbox.quit()

if __name__ == '__main__':
    parser = argparse.ArgumentParser(description='Email Download
Example')
    parser.add_argument('--username', action="store", dest="username",
default=getpass.getuser())
    given_args = parser.parse_args()
    username = given_args.username
    download_email(username)
```

If you run this script, you will see an output similar to the following one. The message is truncated for the sake of privacy.

```
$ python 5_4_download_google_email_via_pop3.py --username=<USERNAME>
Enter your Google password:
Total emails: 333
Getting last message
...[TRUNCATED]
```

How it works...

This recipe downloads a user's first Google message via POP3. The `download_email()` method creates a `mailbox` object with Python, the `POP3_SSL()` class of `poplib`. We passed the Google POP3 server and port address to the class constructor. The `mailbox` object then sets up a user account with the `user()` method call. The password is collected from the user securely using the `getpass` module's `getpass()` method and then passed to the `mailbox` object. The mailbox's `list()` method gives us the e-mail messages as a Python list.

This script first displays the number of e-mail messages stored in the mailbox and retrieves the first message with the `retr()` method call. Finally, it's safe to call the `quit()` method on the mailbox to clean up the connection.

Checking your remote e-mail with IMAP

Instead of using POP3, you can also use IMAP to retrieve the e-mail message from your Google account. In this case, the message won't be deleted after retrieval.

Getting ready

To run this recipe, you should have an e-mail account with Google or any other service provider.

How to do it...

Let us connect to your Google e-mail account and read the first e-mail message. If you don't delete it, the first e-mail message would be the welcome message from Google.

Listing 5.5 shows us how to check Google e-mail with IMAP as follows:

```
#!/usr/bin/env python
# Python Network Programming Cookbook -- Chapter - 5
# This program is optimized for Python 2.7.
# It may run on any other version with/without modifications.

import argparse
import getpass
import imaplib
GOOGLE_IMAP_SERVER = 'imap.googlemail.com'
def check_email(username):
    mailbox = imaplib.IMAP4_SSL(GOOGLE_IMAP_SERVER, '993')
    password = getpass.getpass(prompt="Enter you Google password: ")
    mailbox.login(username, password)
    mailbox.select('Inbox')
    typ, data = mailbox.search(None, 'ALL')
    for num in data[0].split():
        typ, data = mailbox.fetch(num, '(RFC822)')

        print 'Message %s\n%s\n' % (num, data[0][1])
        break
    mailbox.close()
    mailbox.logout()
if __name__ == '__main__':
    parser = argparse.ArgumentParser(description='Email Download 
Example')
    parser.add_argument('--username', action="store", dest="username", 
default=getpass.getuser())
    given_args = parser.parse_args()
    username = given_args.username
    check_email(username)
```

If you run this script, this will show the following output. In order to remove the private part of the data, we truncated some user data.

```
$$ python 5_5_check_remote_email_via_imap.py --username=<USER_NAME>
Enter your Google password:
Message 1
Received: by 10.140.142.16; Sat, 17 Nov 2007 09:26:31 -0800 (PST)
Message-ID: <...>@mail.gmail.com>
Date: Sat, 17 Nov 2007 09:26:31 -0800
From: "Gmail Team" <mail-noreply@google.com>
To: "<User Full Name>" <USER_NAME>@gmail.com>
Subject: Gmail is different. Here's what you need to know.
MIME-Version: 1.0
Content-Type: multipart/alternative;
    boundary="----=_Part_7453_30339499.1195320391988"

------=_Part_7453_30339499.1195320391988
Content-Type: text/plain; charset=ISO-8859-1
Content-Transfer-Encoding: 7bit
Content-Disposition: inline

Messages that are easy to find, an inbox that organizes itself, great
spam-fighting tools and built-in chat. Sound cool? Welcome to Gmail.

To get started, you may want to:
[TRUNCATED]
```

How it works...

The preceding script takes a Google username from the command line and calls the `check_email()` function. This function creates an IMAP mailbox with the `IMAP4_SSL()` class of `imaplib`, which is initialized with Google's IMAP server and default port.

Then, this function logs in to the mailbox with a password, which is captured by the `getpass()` method of the `getpass` module. The inbox folder is selected by calling the `select()` method on the `mailbox` object.

The `mailbox` object has many useful methods. Two of them are `search()` and `fetch()` that are used to get the first e-mail message. Finally, it's safer to call the `close()` and `logout()` method on the `mailbox` object to end the IMAP connection.

Sending an e-mail with an attachment via Gmail SMTP server

You would like to send an e-mail message from your Google e-mail account to another account. You also need to attach a file with this message.

Getting ready

To run this recipe, you should have an e-mail account with Google or any other service provider.

How to do it...

We can create an e-mail message and attach Python's `python-logo.gif` file with the e-mail message. Then, this message is sent from a Google account to a different account.

Listing 4.6 shows us how to send an e-mail from your Google account:

```
#!/usr/bin/env python
# Python Network Programming Cookbook -- Chapter - 5
# This program is optimized for Python 2.7.
# It may run on any other version with/without modifications.

import argparse
import os
import getpass
import re
import sys
import smtplib

from email.mime.image import MIMEImage
from email.mime.multipart import MIMEMultipart
from email.mime.text import MIMEText

SMTP_SERVER = 'smtp.gmail.com'
SMTP_PORT = 587

def send_email(sender, recipient):
    """ Send email message """
    msg = MIMEMultipart()
    msg['Subject'] = 'Python Email Test'
    msg['To'] = recipient
    msg['From'] = sender
    subject = 'Python email Test'
    message = 'Images attached.'
    # attach image files
```

```
    files = os.listdir(os.getcwd())
    gifsearch = re.compile(".gif", re.IGNORECASE)
    files = filter(gifsearch.search, files)
    for filename in files:
        path = os.path.join(os.getcwd(), filename)
        if not os.path.isfile(path):
            continue
        img = MIMEImage(open(path, 'rb').read(), _subtype="gif")

        img.add_header('Content-Disposition', 'attachment', 
filename=filename)
        msg.attach(img)

    part = MIMEText('text', "plain")
    part.set_payload(message)
    msg.attach(part)

    # create smtp session
    session = smtplib.SMTP(SMTP_SERVER, SMTP_PORT)
    session.ehlo()
    session.starttls()
    session.ehlo
    password = getpass.getpass(prompt="Enter you Google password: ")
    session.login(sender, password)
    session.sendmail(sender, recipient, msg.as_string())
    print "Email sent."
    session.quit()

if __name__ == '__main__':
    parser = argparse.ArgumentParser(description='Email Sending 
Example')
    parser.add_argument('--sender', action="store", dest="sender")
    parser.add_argument('--recipient', action="store", 
dest="recipient")
    given_args = parser.parse_args()
    send_email(given_args.sender, given_args.recipient)
```

Running the following script outputs the success of sending an e-mail to any e-mail address if you provide your Google account details correctly. After running this script, you can check your recipient e-mail account to verify that the e-mail is actually sent.

```
$ python 5_6_send_email_from_gmail.py --sender=<USERNAME>@gmail.com –
recipient=<USER>@<ANOTHER_COMPANY.com>
Enter you Google password:
Email sent.
```

How it works...

In this recipe, an e-mail message is created in the `send_email()` function. This function is supplied with a Google account from where the e-mail message will be sent. The message header object, `msg`, is created by calling the `MIMEMultipart()` class and then subject, recipient, and sender information is added on it.

Python's regular expression-handling module is used to filter the `.gif` image on the current path. The image attachment object, `img`, is then created with the `MIMEImage()` method from the `email.mime.image` module. A correct image header is added to this object and finally, the image is attached with the `msg` object created earlier. We can attach multiple image files within a `for` loop as shown in this recipe. We can also attach a plain text attachment in a similar way.

To send the e-mail message, we create an SMTP session. We call some testing method on this session object, such as `ehlo()` or `starttls()`. Then, log in to the Google SMTP server with a username and password and a `sendmail()` method is called to send the e-mail.

Writing a guestbook for your (Python-based) web server with CGI

Common Gateway Interface (**CGI**) is a standard in web programming by which custom scripts can be used to produce web server output. You would like to catch the HTML form input from a user's browser, redirect it to another page, and acknowledge a user action.

How to do it...

We first need to run a web server that supports CGI scripts. We placed our Python CGI script inside a `cgi-bin/` subdirectory and then visited the HTML page that contains the feedback form. Upon submitting this form, our web server will send the form data to the CGI script, and we'll see the output produced by this script.

Listing 5.7 shows us how the Python web server supports CGI:

```
#!/usr/bin/env python
# Python Network Programming Cookbook -- Chapter - 5
# This program is optimized for Python 2.7.
# It may run on any other version with/without modifications.

import os
import cgi
import argparse
import BaseHTTPServer
import CGIHTTPServer
import cgitb
cgitb.enable()  ## enable CGI error reporting
```

```
def web_server(port):
    server = BaseHTTPServer.HTTPServer
    handler = CGIHTTPServer.CGIHTTPRequestHandler #RequestsHandler
    server_address = ("", port)
    handler.cgi_directories = ["/cgi-bin", ]
    httpd = server(server_address, handler)
    print "Starting web server with CGI support on port: %s ..." %port
    httpd.serve_forever()
if __name__ == '__main__':
    parser = argparse.ArgumentParser(description='CGI Server Example')
    parser.add_argument('--port', action="store", dest="port",
type=int, required=True)
    given_args = parser.parse_args()
    web_server(given_args.port)
```

The following screenshot shows CGI enabled web server is serving contents:

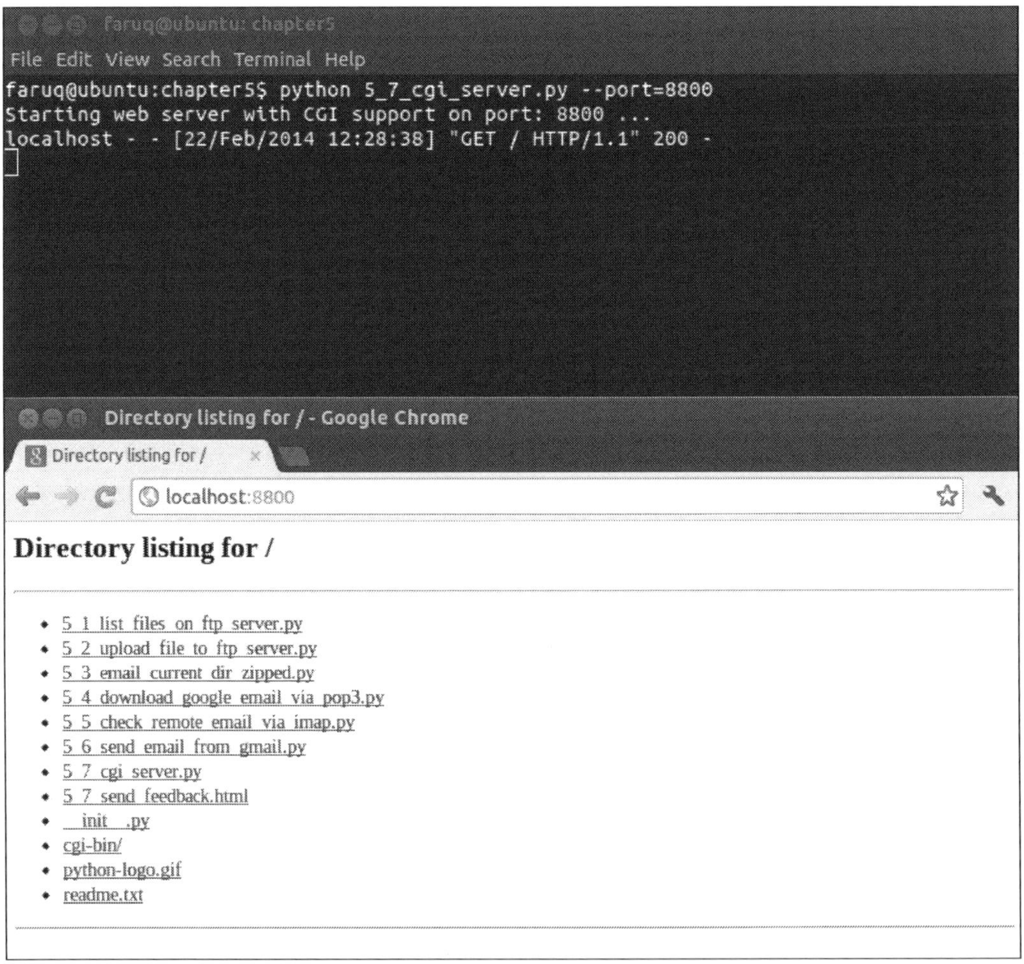

If you run this recipe, you will see the following output:

```
$ python 5_7_cgi_server.py --port=8800
Starting web server with CGI support on port: 8800 ...
localhost - - [19/May/2013 18:40:22] "GET / HTTP/1.1" 200 -
```

Now, you need to visit `http://localhost:8800/5_7_send_feedback.html` from your browser.

You will see an input form. We assume that you provide the following input to this form:

```
Name:   User1
Comment: Comment1
```

The following screenshot shows the entering user comment in a web form:

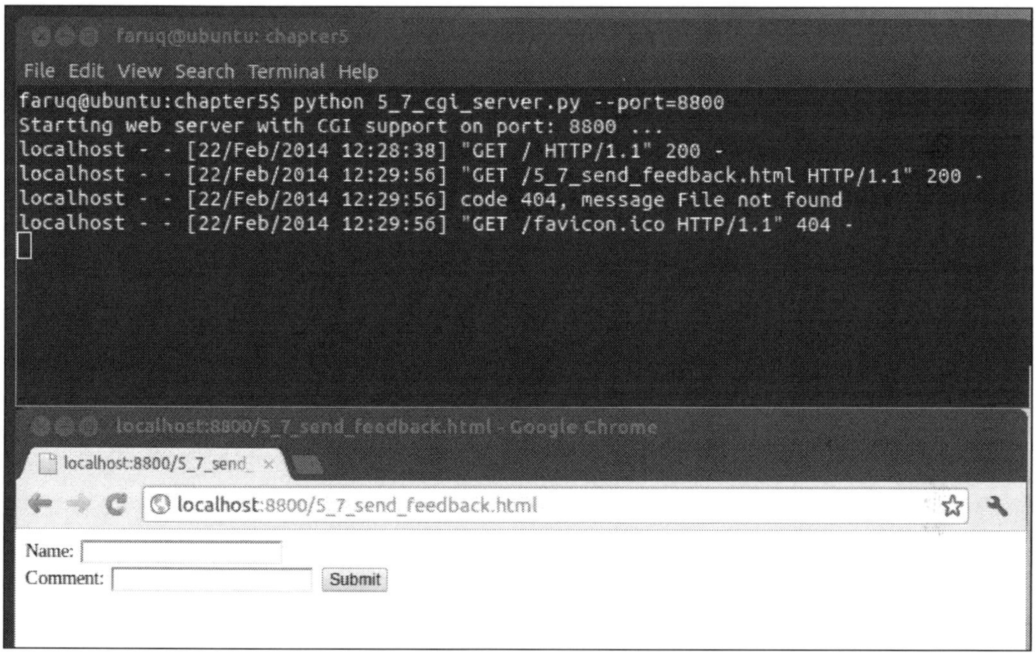

Then, your browser will be redirected to `http://localhost:8800/cgi-bin/5_7_get_feedback.py` where you can see the following output:

```
User1 sends a comment: Comment1
```

The user comment is shown in the browser:

How it works...

We have used a basic HTTP server setup that can handle CGI requests. Python provides these interfaces in the `BaseHTTPServer` and `CGIHTTPserver` modules.

The handler is configured to use the `/cgi-bin` path to launch the CGI scripts. No other path can be used to run the CGI scripts.

The HTML feedback form located on `5_7_send_feedback.html` shows a very basic HTML form containing the following code:

```
<html>
   <body>
         <form action="/cgi-bin/5_7_get_feedback.py" method="post">
                Name: <input type="text" name="Name">  <br />
                Comment: <input type="text" name="Comment" />
                <input type="submit" value="Submit" />
         </form>
   </body>
</html>
```

Note that the form method is `POST` and action is set to the `/cgi-bin/5_7_get_feedback.py` file. The contents of this file are as follows:

```
#!/usr/bin/env python
# Python Network Programming Cookbook -- Chapter - 5
# This program requires Python 2.7 or any later version
import cgi
import cgitb
# Create instance of FieldStorage
form = cgi.FieldStorage()
```

```
# Get data from fields
name = form.getvalue('Name')
comment  = form.getvalue('Comment')
print "Content-type:text/html\r\n\r\n"
print "<html>"
print "<head>"
print "<title>CGI Program Example </title>"
print "</head>"
print "<body>"
print "<h2> %s sends a comment: %s</h2>" % (name, comment)
print "</body>"
print "</html>"
```

In this CGI script, the `FieldStorage()` method is called from `cgilib`. This returns a form object to process the HTML form inputs. Two inputs are parsed here (`name` and `comment`) using the `getvalue()` method. Finally, the script acknowledges the user input by echoing a line back saying that the user x has sent a comment.

6
Screen-scraping and Other Practical Applications

In this chapter, we will cover the following topics:

- Searching for business addresses using the Google Maps API
- Searching for geographic coordinates using the Google Maps URL
- Searching for an article in Wikipedia
- Searching for Google stock quote
- Searching for a source code repository at GitHub
- Reading news feed from BBC
- Crawling links present in a web page

Introduction

This chapter shows some of the interesting Python scripts that you can write to extract useful information from the web, for example, searching for a business address, stock quote for a particular company or the latest news from a news agency website. These scripts demonstrate how Python can extract simple information in simpler ways without communicating with complex APIs.

Following these recipes, you should be able to write code for complex scenarios, for example, find the details about a business, including location, news, stock quote, and so on.

Searching for business addresses using the Google Maps API

You would like to search for the address of a well-known business in your area.

Getting ready

You can use the Python geocoding library `pygeocoder` to search for a local business. You need to install this library from **PyPI** with `pip` or `easy_install`, by entering `$ pip install pygeocoder` or `$ easy_install pygeocoder`.

How to do it...

Let us find the address of Argos Ltd., a well-known UK retailer using a few lines of Python code.

Listing 6.1 gives a simple geocoding example to search for a business address, as follows:

```
#!/usr/bin/env python

# Python Network Programming Cookbook -- Chapter - 6
# This program is optimized for Python 2.7.
# It may run on any other version with/without modifications.

from pygeocoder import Geocoder

def search_business(business_name):

  results = Geocoder.geocode(business_name)

  for result in results:
    print result

if __name__ == '__main__':
  business_name =  "Argos Ltd, London"
  print "Searching %s" %business_name
  search_business(business_name)
```

This recipe will print the address of Argos Ltd., as shown. The output may vary slightly based on the output from your installed geocoding library:

```
$ python 6_1_search_business_addr.py
Searching Argos Ltd, London

Argos Ltd, 110-114 King Street, London, Greater London W6 0QP, UK
```

How it works...

This recipe relies on the Python third-party geocoder library.

This recipe defines a simple function `search_business()` that takes the business name as an input and passes that to the `geocode()` function. The `geocode()` function can return zero or more search results depending on your search term.

In this recipe, the `geocode()` function has got the business name Argos Ltd., London, as the search query. In return, it gives the address of Argos Ltd., which is 110-114 King Street, London, Greater London W6 0QP, UK.

See also

The `pygeocoder` library is powerful and has many interesting and useful features for geocoding. You may find more details on the developer's website at `https://bitbucket.org/xster/pygeocoder/wiki/Home`.

Searching for geographic coordinates using the Google Maps URL

Sometimes you'd like to have a simple function that gives the geographic coordinates of a city by giving it just the name of that city. You may not be interested in installing any third-party libraries for this simple task.

How to do it...

In this simple screen-scraping example, we use the Google Maps URL to query the latitude and longitude of a city. The URL used to query can be found after making a custom search on the Google Maps page. We can perform the following steps to extract some information from Google Maps.

Let us take the name of a city from the command line using the `argparse` module.

We can open the maps search URL using the `urlopen()` function of `urllib`. This will give an XML output if the URL is correct.

Now, process the XML output in order to get the geographic coordinates of that city.

Listing 6.2 helps finding the geographic coordinates of a city using Google Maps, as shown:

```
#!/usr/bin/env python
# Python Network Programming Cookbook -- Chapter - 6
# This program is optimized for Python 2.7.
# It may run on any other version with/without modifications.
```

```
import argparse
import os
import urllib

ERROR_STRING = '<error>'

def find_lat_long(city):
  """ Find geographic coordinates """
  # Encode query string into Google maps URL
    url = 'http://maps.google.com/?q=' + urllib.quote(city) +
'&output=js'
    print 'Query: %s' % (url)

  # Get XML location from Google maps
    xml = urllib.urlopen(url).read()

    if ERROR_STRING in xml:
      print '\nGoogle cannot interpret the city.'
      return
    else:
    # Strip lat/long coordinates from XML
      lat,lng = 0.0,0.0
      center =
xml[xml.find('{center')+10:xml.find('}',xml.find('{center'))]
      center = center.replace('lat:','').replace('lng:','')
      lat,lng = center.split(',')
      print "Latitude/Longitude: %s/%s\n" %(lat, lng)


    if __name__ == '__main__':
      parser = argparse.ArgumentParser(description='City Geocode
Search')
      parser.add_argument('--city', action="store", dest="city",
required=True)
      given_args = parser.parse_args()

      print "Finding geographic coordinates of %s"
%given_args.city
      find_lat_long(given_args.city)
```

If you run this script, you should see something similar to the following:

```
$ python 6_2_geo_coding_by_google_maps.py --city=London
Finding geograhic coordinates of London
Query: http://maps.google.com/?q=London&output=js
Latitude/Longitude: 51.511214000000002/-0.119824
```

How it works...

This recipe takes a name of a city from the command line and passes that to the `find_lat_long()` function. This function queries the Google Maps service using the `urlopen()` function of `urllib` and gets the XML output. Then, the error string '<error>' is searched for. If that's not present, it means there are some good results.

If you print out the raw XML, it's a long stream of characters produced for the browser. In the browser, it would be interesting to display the layers in maps. But in our case, we just need the latitude and longitude.

From the raw XML, the latitude and longitude is extracted using the string method `find()`. This searches for the keyword "center". This list key possesses the geographic coordinates information. But it also contains the additional characters which are removed using the string method `replace()`.

You may try this recipe to find out the latitude/longitude of any known city of the world.

Searching for an article in Wikipedia

Wikipedia is a great site to gather information about virtually anything, for example, people, places, technology, and what not. If you like to search for something on Wikipedia from your Python script, this recipe is for you.

Here is an example:

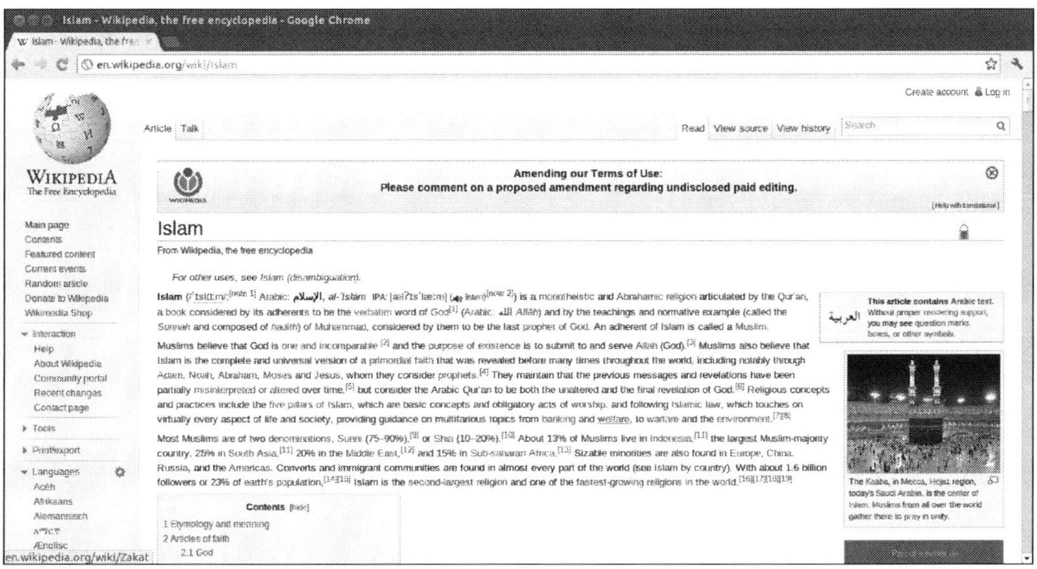

Getting ready

You need to install the `pyyaml` third-party library from PyPI using `pip` or `easy_install` by entering `$ pip install pyyaml` or `$ easy_install pyyaml`.

How to do it...

Let us search for the keyword `Islam` in Wikipedia and print each search result in one line.

Listing 6.3 explains how to search for an article in Wikipedia, as shown:

```
#!/usr/bin/env python
# -*- coding: utf-8 -*-
# Python Network Programming Cookbook -- Chapter - 6
# This program is optimized for Python 2.7.
# It may run on any other version with/without modifications

import argparse
import re
import yaml
import urllib
import urllib2

SEARCH_URL = 'http://%s.wikipedia.org/w/api.php?action=query&list=sear
ch&srsearch=%s&sroffset=%d&srlimit=%d&format=yaml'

class Wikipedia:

  def __init__(self, lang='en'):
    self.lang = lang

  def _get_content(self, url):
    request = urllib2.Request(url)
    request.add_header('User-Agent', 'Mozilla/20.0')

    try:
      result = urllib2.urlopen(request)
      except urllib2.HTTPError, e:
        print "HTTP Error:%s" %(e.reason)
      except Exception, e:
        print "Error occurred: %s" %str(e)
      return result

  def search_content(self, query, page=1, limit=10):
    offset = (page - 1) * limit
```

```
        url = SEARCH_URL % (self.lang, urllib.quote_plus(query),
    offset, limit)
        content = self._get_content(url).read()

        parsed = yaml.load(content)
        search = parsed['query']['search']
        if not search:
        return

        results = []
        for article in search:
          snippet = article['snippet']
          snippet = re.sub(r'(?m)<.*?>', '', snippet)
          snippet = re.sub(r'\s+', ' ', snippet)
          snippet = snippet.replace(' . ', '. ')
          snippet = snippet.replace(' , ', ', ')
          snippet = snippet.strip()

        results.append({
          'title' : article['title'].strip(),
    'snippet' : snippet
        })

        return results

    if __name__ == '__main__':
      parser = argparse.ArgumentParser(description='Wikipedia search')
      parser.add_argument('--query', action="store", dest="query",
    required=True)
      given_args = parser.parse_args()

      wikipedia = Wikipedia()
      search_term = given_args.query
      print "Searching Wikipedia for %s" %search_term
      results = wikipedia.search_content(search_term)
      print "Listing %s search results..." %len(results)
      for result in results:
        print "==%s== \n \t%s" %(result['title'], result['snippet'])
      print "---- End of search results ----"
```

Running this recipe to query Wikipedia about Islam shows the following output:

```
$ python 6_3_search_article_in_wikipedia.py --query='Islam'
Searching Wikipedia for Islam
Listing 10 search results...
==Islam==
```

```
    Islam. (ˈ | ɪ | s | l | ɑː | m الإسلام, ar | ALA | al-ˈIslām
ælʔɪsˈlæːm | IPA | ar-al_islam. ...


==Sunni Islam==
    Sunni Islam (ˈ | s | uː | n | i or ˈ | s | ʊ | n | i |) is the
largest branch of Islam ; its adherents are referred to in Arabic as ...
==Muslim==
    A Muslim, also spelled Moslem is an adherent of Islam, a
monotheistic Abrahamic religion based on the Qur'an —which Muslims
consider the ...
==Sharia==
    is the moral code and religious law of Islam. Sharia deals with
many topics addressed by secular law, including crime, politics, and ...
==History of Islam==
    The history of Islam concerns the Islamic religion and its
adherents, known as Muslim s. " "Muslim" is an Arabic word meaning
"one who ...


==Caliphate==
    a successor to Islamic prophet Muhammad ) and all the Prophets
of Islam. The term caliphate is often applied to successions of
Muslim ...
==Islamic fundamentalism==
    Islamic ideology and is a group of religious ideologies seen as
advocating a return to the "fundamentals" of Islam : the Quran and
the Sunnah. ...
==Islamic architecture==
    Islamic architecture encompasses a wide range of both secular
and religious styles from the foundation of Islam to the present day. ...
---- End of search results ----
```

How it works...

First, we collect the Wikipedia URL template for searching an article. We created a class called `Wikipedia`, which has two methods: `_get_content()` and `search_content()`. By default upon initialization, the class sets up its language attribute `lang` to `en` (English).

The command-line query string is passed to the `search_content()` method. It then constructs the actual search URL by inserting variables such as language, query string, page offset, and number of results to return. The `search_content()` method can optionally take the parameters and the offset is determined by the `(page -1) * limit` expression.

The content of the search result is fetched via the `_get_content()` method which calls the `urlopen()` function of `urllib`. In the search URL, we set up the result format `yaml`, which is basically intended for plain text files. The `yaml` search result is then parsed with Python's `pyyaml` library.

The search result is processed by substituting the regular expressions found in each result item. For example, the `re.sub(r'(?m)<.*?>', '', snippet)` expression takes the snippet string and replaces a raw pattern `(?m)<.*?>)`. To learn more about regular expressions, visit the Python document page, available at `http://docs.python.org/2/howto/regex.html`.

In Wikipedia terminology, each article has a snippet or a short description. We create a list of dictionary items where each item contains the title and the snippet of each search result. The results are printed on the screen by looping through this list of dictionary items.

Searching for Google stock quote

If the stock quote of any company is of interest to you, this recipe can help you to find today's stock quote of that company.

Getting ready

We assume that you already know the symbol used by your favorite company to enlist itself on any stock exchange. If you don't know, get the symbol from the company website or just search in Google.

How to do it...

Here, we use Google Finance (`http://finance.google.com/`) to search for the stock quote of a given company. You can input the symbol via the command line, as shown in the next code.

Listing 6.4 describes how to search for Google stock quote, as shown:

```
#!/usr/bin/env python
# Python Network Programming Cookbook -- Chapter - 6
# This program is optimized for Python 2.7.
# It may run on any other version with/without modifications.

import argparse
import urllib
import re
from datetime import datetime
```

```
SEARCH_URL = 'http://finance.google.com/finance?q='

def get_quote(symbol):
  content = urllib.urlopen(SEARCH_URL + symbol).read()
  m = re.search('id="ref_694653_l".*?>(.*?)<', content)
  if m:
    quote = m.group(1)
  else:
    quote = 'No quote available for: ' + symbol
  return quote

if __name__ == '__main__':
  parser = argparse.ArgumentParser(description='Stock quote
search')
  parser.add_argument('--symbol', action="store", dest="symbol",
required=True)
  given_args = parser.parse_args()
  print "Searching stock quote for symbol '%s'" %given_args.symbol
  print "Stock  quote for %s at %s: %s" %(given_args.symbol ,
datetime.today(),  get_quote(given_args.symbol))
```

If you run this script, you will see an output similar to the following. Here, the stock quote for Google is searched by inputting the symbol `goog`, as shown:

```
$ python 6_4_google_stock_quote.py --symbol=goog
Searching stock quote for symbol 'goog'
Stock quote for goog at 2013-08-20 18:50:29.483380: 868.86
```

How it works...

This recipe uses the `urlopen()` function of `urllib` to get the stock data from the Google Finance website.

By using the regular expression library `re`, it locates the stock quote data in the first group of items. The `search()` function of `re` is powerful enough to search the content and filter the ID data of that particular company.

Using this recipe, we searched for the stock quote of Google, which was `868.86` on August 20, 2013.

Searching for a source code repository at GitHub

As a Python programmer, you may already be familiar with GitHub (`http://www.github.com`), a source code-sharing website, as shown in the following screenshot. You can share your source code privately to a team or publicly to the world using GitHub. It has a nice API interface to query about any source code repository. This recipe may give you a starting point to create your own source code search engine.

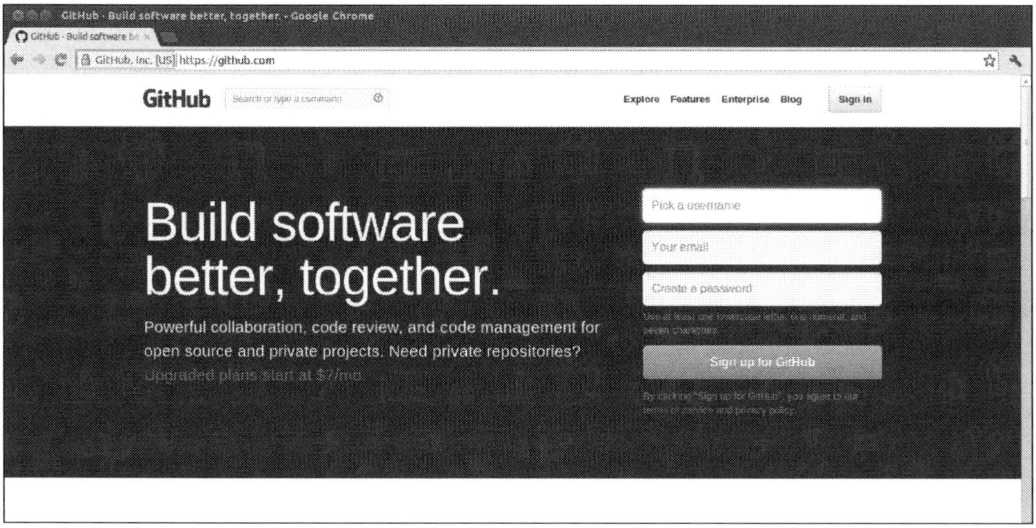

Getting ready

To run this recipe, you need to install the third-party Python library `requests` by entering `$ pip install requests` or `$ easy_install requests`.

How to do it...

We would like to define a `search_repository()` function that will take the name of author (also known as coder), repository, and search key. In return, it will give us back the available result against the search key. From the GitHub API, the following are the available search keys: `issues_url`, `has_wiki`, `forks_url`, `mirror_url`, `subscription_url`, `notifications_url`, `collaborators_url`, `updated_at`, `private`, `pulls_url`, `issue_comment_url`, `labels_url`, `full_name`, `owner`, `statuses_url`, `id`, `keys_url`, `description`, `tags_url`, `network_count`, `downloads_url`, `assignees_url`, `contents_url`, `git_refs_url`, `open_issues_count`, `clone_url`, `watchers_count`, `git_tags_url`, `milestones_url`, `languages_url`, `size`, `homepage`, `fork`, `commits_url`, `issue_events_url`, `archive_url`, `comments_url`, `events_url`, `contributors_url`, `html_url`, `forks`, `compare_url`, `open_issues`, `git_url`, `svn_url`, `merges_url`, `has_issues`, `ssh_url`, `blobs_url`, `master_branch`, `git_commits_url`, `hooks_url`, `has_downloads`, `watchers`, `name`, `language`, `url`, `created_at`, `pushed_at`, `forks_count`, `default_branch`, `teams_url`, `trees_url`, `organization`, `branches_url`, `subscribers_url`, and `stargazers_url`.

Listing 6.5 gives the code to search for details of a source code repository at GitHub, as shown:

```
#!/usr/bin/env python
# Python Network Programming Cookbook -- Chapter - 6
# This program is optimized for Python 2.7.
# It may run on any other version with/without modifications.

SEARCH_URL_BASE = 'https://api.github.com/repos'

import argparse
import requests
import json

def search_repository(author, repo, search_for='homepage'):
  url = "%s/%s/%s" %(SEARCH_URL_BASE, author, repo)
  print "Searching Repo URL: %s" %url
  result = requests.get(url)
  if(result.ok):
    repo_info = json.loads(result.text or result.content)
    print "Github repository info for: %s" %repo
    result = "No result found!"
    keys = []
    for key,value in repo_info.iteritems():
      if  search_for in key:
          result = value
      return result
```

```
if __name__ == '__main__':
  parser = argparse.ArgumentParser(description='Github search')
  parser.add_argument('--author', action="store", dest="author",
required=True)
  parser.add_argument('--repo', action="store", dest="repo",
required=True)
  parser.add_argument('--search_for', action="store",
dest="search_for", required=True)

  given_args = parser.parse_args()
  result = search_repository(given_args.author, given_args.repo,
given_args.search_for)
  if isinstance(result, dict):
    print "Got result for '%s'..." %(given_args.search_for)
    for key,value in result.iteritems():
    print "%s => %s" %(key,value)
  else:
    print "Got result for %s: %s" %(given_args.search_for,
result)
```

If you run this script to search for the owner of the Python web framework Django, you can get the following result:

```
$ python 6_5_search_code_github.py --author=django --repo=django
--search_for=owner
Searching Repo URL: https://api.github.com/repos/django/django
Github repository info for: django
Got result for 'owner'...
following_url => https://api.github.com/users/django/following{/other_
user}
events_url => https://api.github.com/users/django/events{/privacy}
organizations_url => https://api.github.com/users/django/orgs
url => https://api.github.com/users/django
gists_url => https://api.github.com/users/django/gists{/gist_id}
html_url => https://github.com/django
subscriptions_url => https://api.github.com/users/django/subscriptions
avatar_url => https://1.gravatar.com/avatar/fd542381031aa84dca86628ece84f
c07?d=https%3A%2F%2Fidenticons.github.com%2Fe94df919e51ae96652259468415d
4f77.png
repos_url => https://api.github.com/users/django/repos
received_events_url => https://api.github.com/users/django/received_
events
```

```
gravatar_id => fd542381031aa84dca86628ece84fc07
starred_url => https://api.github.com/users/django/starred{/owner}{/repo}
login => django
type => Organization
id => 27804
followers_url => https://api.github.com/users/django/followers
```

How it works...

This script takes three command-line arguments: repository author (`--author`), repository name (`--repo`), and the item to search for (`--search_for`). The arguments are processed by the `argpase` module.

Our `search_repository()` function appends the command-line arguments to a fixed search URL and receives the content by calling the `requests` module's `get()` function.

The search results are, by default, returned in the JSON format. This content is then processed with the `json` module's `loads()` method. The search key is then looked for inside the result and the corresponding value of that key is returned back to the caller of the `search_repository()` function.

In the main user code, we check whether the search result is an instance of the Python dictionary. If yes, then the key/values are printed iteratively. Otherwise, the value is printed.

Reading news feed from BBC

If you are developing a social networking website with news and stories, you may be interested to present the news from various world news agencies, such as BBC and Reuters. Let us try to read news from BBC via a Python script.

Getting ready

This recipe relies on Python's third-party `feedparser` library. You can install this by running the following command:

```
$ pip install feedparser
```

Or

```
$ easy_install feedparser
```

How to do it...

First, we collect the BBC's news feed URL from the BBC website. This URL can be used as a template to search news on various types, such as world, UK, health, business, and technology. So, we can take the type of news to display as user input. Then, we depend on the `read_news()` function, which will fetch the news from the BBC.

Listing 6.6 explains how to read news feed from the BBC, as shown in the following code:

```
#!/usr/bin/env python
# Python Network Programming Cookbook -- Chapter - 6
# This program is optimized for Python 2.7.
# It may run on any other version with/without modifications.


from datetime import datetime
import feedparser
BBC_FEED_URL = 'http://feeds.bbci.co.uk/news/%s/rss.xml'

def read_news(feed_url):
  try:
    data = feedparser.parse(feed_url)
  except Exception, e:
    print "Got error: %s" %str(e)

  for entry in data.entries:
    print(entry.title)
    print(entry.link)
    print(entry.description)
    print("\n")

if __name__ == '__main__':
  print "==== Reading technology news feed from bbc.co.uk
(%s)====" %datetime.today()

  print "Enter the type of news feed: "
  print "Available options are: world, uk, health, sci-tech,
business, technology"
  type = raw_input("News feed type:")
  read_news(BBC_FEED_URL %type)
  print "==== End of BBC news feed ====="
```

Running this script will show you the available news categories. If we choose technology as the category, you can get the latest news on technology, as shown in the following command:

```
$ python 6_6_read_bbc_news_feed.py
==== Reading technology news feed from bbc.co.uk (2013-08-20 19:02:33.940014)====
Enter the type of news feed:
Available options are: world, uk, health, sci-tech, business, technology
News feed type:technology
Xbox One courts indie developers
http://www.bbc.co.uk/news/technology-23765453#sa-ns_mchannel=rss&ns_source=PublicRSS20-sa
Microsoft is to give away free Xbox One development kits to encourage independent developers to self-publish games for its forthcoming console.


Fast in-flight wi-fi by early 2014
http://www.bbc.co.uk/news/technology-23768536#sa-ns_mchannel=rss&ns_source=PublicRSS20-sa
Passengers on planes, trains and ships may soon be able to take advantage of high-speed wi-fi connections, says Ofcom.


Anonymous 'hacks council website'
http://www.bbc.co.uk/news/uk-england-surrey-23772635#sa-ns_mchannel=rss&ns_source=PublicRSS20-sa
A Surrey council blames hackers Anonymous after references to a Guardian journalist's partner detained at Heathrow Airport appear on its website.


Amazon.com website goes offline
http://www.bbc.co.uk/news/technology-23762526#sa-ns_mchannel=rss&ns_source=PublicRSS20-sa
Amazon's US website goes offline for about half an hour, the latest high-profile internet firm to face such a problem in recent days.


[TRUNCATED]
```

How it works...

In this recipe, the `read_news()` function relies on Python's third-party module `feedparser`. The `feedparser` module's `parser()` method returns the feed data in a structured fashion.

In this recipe, the `parser()` method parses the given feed URL. This URL is constructed from `BBC_FEED_URL` and user input.

After some valid feed data is obtained by calling `parse()`, the contents of the data is then printed, such as title, link, and description, of each feed entry.

Crawling links present in a web page

At times you would like to find a specific keyword present in a web page. In a web browser, you can use the browser's in-page search facility to locate the terms. Some browsers can highlight it. In a complex situation, you would like to dig deep and follow every URL present in a web page and find that specific term. This recipe will automate that task for you.

How to do it...

Let us write a `search_links()` function that will take three arguments: the search URL, the depth of the recursive search, and the search key/term, since every URL may have links present in the content and that content may have more URLs to crawl. To limit the recursive search, we define a depth. Upon reaching that depth, no more recursive search will be done.

Listing 6.7 gives the code for crawling links present in a web page, as shown in the following code:

```
#!/usr/bin/env python
# Python Network Programming Cookbook -- Chapter - 6
# This program is optimized for Python 2.7.
# It may run on any other version with/without modifications.

import argparse
import sys
import httplib
import re

processed = []

def search_links(url, depth, search):
  # Process http links that are not processed yet
  url_is_processed = (url in processed)
  if (url.startswith("http://") and (not url_is_processed)):
    processed.append(url)
    url = host = url.replace("http://", "", 1)
    path = "/"

    urlparts = url.split("/")
    if (len(urlparts) > 1):
```

```
        host = urlparts[0]
        path = url.replace(host, "", 1)

       # Start crawling
       print "Crawling URL path:%s%s " %(host, path)
       conn = httplib.HTTPConnection(host)
       req = conn.request("GET", path)
       result = conn.getresponse()

      # find the links
      contents = result.read()
      all_links = re.findall('href="(.*?)"', contents)

      if (search in contents):
        print "Found " + search + " at " + url

        print " ==> %s: processing %s links" %(str(depth),
str(len(all_links)))
        for href in all_links:
        # Find relative urls
        if (href.startswith("/")):
          href = "http://" + host + href

          # Recurse links
          if (depth > 0):
            search_links(href, depth-1, search)
      else:
        print "Skipping link: %s ..." %url


if __name__ == '__main__':
  parser = argparse.ArgumentParser(description='Webpage link
crawler')
  parser.add_argument('--url', action="store", dest="url",
required=True)
  parser.add_argument('--query', action="store", dest="query",
required=True)
  parser.add_argument('--depth', action="store", dest="depth",
default=2)

  given_args = parser.parse_args()

  try:
    search_links(given_args.url,
given_args.depth,given_args.query)
    except KeyboardInterrupt:
      print "Aborting search by user request."
```

If you run this script to search `www.python.org` for `python`, you will see an output similar to the following:

```
$ python 6_7_python_link_crawler.py --url='http://python.org'
--query='python'
Crawling URL path:python.org/
Found python at python.org
 ==> 2: processing 123 links
Crawling URL path:www.python.org/channews.rdf
Found python at www.python.org/channews.rdf
 ==> 1: processing 30 links
Crawling URL path:www.python.org/download/releases/3.4.0/
Found python at www.python.org/download/releases/3.4.0/
 ==> 0: processing 111 links
Skipping link: https://ep2013.europython.eu/blog/2013/05/15/epc20145-
call-proposals ...
Crawling URL path:www.python.org/download/releases/3.2.5/
Found python at www.python.org/download/releases/3.2.5/
 ==> 0: processing 113 links
...
Skipping link: http://www.python.org/download/releases/3.2.4/ ...
Crawling URL path:wiki.python.org/moin/WikiAttack2013
^CAborting search by user request.
```

How it works...

This recipe can take three command-line inputs: search URL (`--url`), the query string (`--query`), and the depth of recursion (`--depth`). These inputs are processed by the `argparse` module.

When the `search_links()` function is called with the previous arguments, this will recursively iterate on all the links found on that given web page. If it takes too long to finish, you would like to exit prematurely. For this reason, the `search_links()` function is placed inside a try-catch block which can catch the user's keyboard interrupt action, such as *Ctrl* + *C*.

The `search_links()` function keeps track of visited links via a list called `processed`. This is made global to give access to all the recursive function calls.

In a single instance of search, it is ensured that only HTTP URLs are processed in order to avoid the potential SSL certificate errors. The URL is split into a host and a path. The main crawling is initiated using the `HTTPConnection()` function of `httplib`. It gradually makes a `GET` request and a response is then processed using the regular expression module `re`. This collects all the links from the response. Each response is then examined for the search term. If the search term is found, it prints that incident.

The collected links are visited recursively in the same way. If any relative URL is found, that instance is converted into a full URL by prefixing `http://` to the host and the path. If the depth of search is greater than 0, the recursion is activated. It reduces the depth by 1 and runs the search function again. When the search depth becomes 0, the recursion ends.

7
Programming Across Machine Boundaries

In this chapter, we will cover the following recipes:

- Executing a remote shell command using telnet
- Copying a file to a remote machine by SFTP
- Printing a remote machine's CPU information
- Installing a Python package remotely
- Running a MySQL command remotely
- Transferring files to a remote machine over SSH
- Configuring Apache remotely to host a website

Introduction

This chapter promotes some interesting Python libraries. The recipes are presented aiming at the system administrators and advanced Python programmers who like to write code that connects to remote systems and executes commands. The chapter begins with lightweight recipes with a built-in Python library, `telnetlib`. It then brings `Paramiko`, a well-known remote access library. Finally, the powerful remote system administration library, `fabric`, is presented. The `fabric` library is loved by developers who regularly script for automatic deployments, for example, deploying web applications or building custom application binaries.

Executing a remote shell command using telnet

If you need to connect an old network switch or router via telnet, you can do so from a Python script instead of using a bash script or an interactive shell. This recipe will create a simple telnet session. It will show you how to execute shell commands to the remote host.

Getting ready

You need to install the telnet server on your machine and ensure that it's up and running. You can use a package manager that is specific to your operating system to install the telnet server package. For example, on Debian/Ubuntu, you can use `apt-get` or `aptitude` to install the `telnetd` package, as shown in the following command:

```
$ sudo apt-get install telnetd
$ telnet localhost
```

How to do it...

Let us define a function that will take a user's login credentials from the command prompt and connect to a telnet server.

Upon successful connection, it will send the Unix `'ls'` command. Then, it will display the output of the command, for example, listing the contents of a directory.

Listing 7.1 shows the code for a telnet session that executes a Unix command remotely as follows:

```
#!/usr/bin/env python
# Python Network Programming Cookbook -- Chapter - 7
# This program is optimized for Python 2.7.
# It may run on any other version with/without modifications.

import getpass
import sys
import telnetlib


def run_telnet_session():
  host = raw_input("Enter remote hostname e.g. localhost:")
  user = raw_input("Enter your remote account: ")
  password = getpass.getpass()

  session = telnetlib.Telnet(host)
```

```
    session.read_until("login: ")
    session.write(user + "\n")
    if password:
      session.read_until("Password: ")
      session.write(password + "\n")

    session.write("ls\n")
    session.write("exit\n")

    print session.read_all()

  if __name__ == '__main__':
    run_telnet_session()
```

If you run a telnet server on your local machine and run this code, it will ask you for your remote user account and password. The following output shows a telnet session executed on a Debian machine:

```
$ python 7_1_execute_remote_telnet_cmd.py
Enter remote hostname e.g. localhost: localhost
Enter your remote account: faruq
Password:

ls
exit
Last login: Mon Aug 12 10:37:10 BST 2013 from localhost on pts/9
Linux debian6 2.6.32-5-686 #1 SMP Mon Feb 25 01:04:36 UTC 2013 i686

The programs included with the Debian GNU/Linux system are free software;
the exact distribution terms for each program are described in the
individual files in /usr/share/doc/*/copyright.

Debian GNU/Linux comes with ABSOLUTELY NO WARRANTY, to the extent
permitted by applicable law.
You have new mail.
faruq@debian6:~$ ls
down                Pictures                Videos
Downloads           projects                yEd
Dropbox             Public
env                 readme.txt
faruq@debian6:~$ exit
logout
```

How it works...

This recipe relies on Python's built-in `telnetlib` networking library to create a telnet session. The `run_telnet_session()` function takes the username and password from the command prompt. The `getpass` module's `getpass()` function is used to get the password as this function won't let you see what is typed on the screen.

In order to create a telnet session, you need to instantiate a `Telnet()` class, which takes a hostname parameter to initialize. In this case, `localhost` is used as the hostname. You can use the `argparse` module to pass a hostname to this script.

The telnet session's remote output can be captured with the `read_until()` method. In the first case, the login prompt is detected using this method. Then, the username with a new line feed is sent to the remote machine by the `write()` method (in this case, the same machine accessed as if it's remote). Similarly, the password was supplied to the remote host.

Then, the `ls` command is sent to be executed. Finally, to disconnect from the remote host, the `exit` command is sent, and all session data received from the remote host is printed on screen using the `read_all()` method.

Copying a file to a remote machine by SFTP

If you want to upload or copy a file from your local machine to a remote machine securely, you can do so via **Secure File Transfer Protocol** (**SFTP**).

Getting ready

This recipe uses a powerful third-party networking library, `Paramiko`, to show you an example of file copying by SFTP, as shown in the following command. You can grab the latest code of `Paramiko` from GitHub (`https://github.com/paramiko/paramiko`) or PyPI:

```
$ pip install paramiko
```

How to do it...

This recipe takes a few command-line inputs: the remote hostname, server port, source filename, and destination filename. For the sake of simplicity, we can use default or hard-coded values for these input parameters.

In order to connect to the remote host, we need the username and password, which can be obtained from the user from the command line.

Listing 7.2 explains how to copy a file remotely by SFTP, as shown in the following code:

```
#!/usr/bin/env python
# Python Network Programming Cookbook -- Chapter - 7
# This program is optimized for Python 2.7.
# It may run on any other version with/without modifications.

import argparse
import paramiko
import getpass


SOURCE = '7_2_copy_remote_file_over_sftp.py'
DESTINATION ='/tmp/7_2_copy_remote_file_over_sftp.py '


def copy_file(hostname, port, username, password, src, dst):
  client = paramiko.SSHClient()
  client.load_system_host_keys()
  print " Connecting to %s \n with username=%s... \n"
%(hostname,username)
  t = paramiko.Transport((hostname, port))
  t.connect(username=username,password=password)
  sftp = paramiko.SFTPClient.from_transport(t)
  print "Copying file: %s to path: %s" %(SOURCE, DESTINATION)
  sftp.put(src, dst)
  sftp.close()
  t.close()


if __name__ == '__main__':
  parser = argparse.ArgumentParser(description='Remote file copy')
  parser.add_argument('--host', action="store", dest="host",
default='localhost')
  parser.add_argument('--port', action="store", dest="port",
default=22, type=int)
  parser.add_argument('--src', action="store", dest="src",
default=SOURCE)
  parser.add_argument('--dst', action="store", dest="dst",
default=DESTINATION)

  given_args = parser.parse_args()
  hostname, port =  given_args.host, given_args.port
  src, dst = given_args.src, given_args.dst

  username = raw_input("Enter the username:")
  password = getpass.getpass("Enter password for %s: " %username)

  copy_file(hostname, port, username, password, src, dst)
```

If you run this script, you will see an output similar to the following:

```
$ python 7_2_copy_remote_file_over_sftp.py
Enter the username:faruq
Enter password for faruq:
 Connecting to localhost
 with username=faruq...
Copying file: 7_2_copy_remote_file_over_sftp.py to path:
/tmp/7_2_copy_remote_file_over_sftp.py
```

How it works...

This recipe can take the various inputs for connecting to a remote machine and copying a file over SFTP.

This recipe passes the command-line input to the `copy_file()` function. It then creates a SSH client calling the `SSHClient` class of `paramiko`. The client needs to load the system host keys. It then connects to the remote system, thus creating an instance of the `transport` class. The actual SFTP connection object, `sftp`, is created by calling the `SFTPClient.from_transport()` function of `paramiko`. This takes the `transport` instance as an input.

After the SFTP connection is ready, the local file is copied over this connection to the remote host using the `put()` method.

Finally, it's a good idea to clean up the SFTP connection and underlying objects by calling the `close()` method separately on each object.

Printing a remote machine's CPU information

Sometimes, we need to run a simple command on a remote machine over SSH. For example, we need to query the remote machine's CPU or RAM information. This can be done from a Python script as shown in this recipe.

Getting ready

You need to install the third-party package, `Paramiko`, as shown in the following command, from the source available from GitHub's repository at `https://github.com/paramiko/paramiko`:

```
$ pip install paramiko
```

How to do it...

We can use the `paramiko` module to create a remote session to a Unix machine.

Then, from this session, we can read the remote machine's `/proc/cpuinfo` file to extract the CPU information.

Listing 7.3 gives the code for printing a remote machine's CPU information, as follows:

```
#!/usr/bin/env python
# Python Network Programming Cookbook -- Chapter - 7
# This program is optimized for Python 2.7.
# It may run on any other version with/without modifications.

import argparse
import getpass
import paramiko

RECV_BYTES = 4096
COMMAND = 'cat /proc/cpuinfo'

def print_remote_cpu_info(hostname, port, username, password):
  client = paramiko.Transport((hostname, port))
  client.connect(username=username, password=password)

  stdout_data = []
  stderr_data = []
  session = client.open_channel(kind='session')
  session.exec_command(COMMAND)
  while True:
    if session.recv_ready():
      stdout_data.append(session.recv(RECV_BYTES))
      if session.recv_stderr_ready():
        stderr_data.append(session.recv_stderr(RECV_BYTES))
      if session.exit_status_ready():
        break

  print 'exit status: ', session.recv_exit_status()
  print ''.join(stdout_data)
  print ''.join(stderr_data)

  session.close()
  client.close()

if __name__ == '__main__':
```

```
    parser = argparse.ArgumentParser(description='Remote file copy')
    parser.add_argument('--host', action="store", dest="host",
default='localhost')
    parser.add_argument('--port', action="store", dest="port",
default=22, type=int)
    given_args = parser.parse_args()
    hostname, port =  given_args.host, given_args.port

    username = raw_input("Enter the username:")
    password = getpass.getpass("Enter password for %s: " %username)
    print_remote_cpu_info(hostname, port, username, password)
```

Running this script will show the CPU information of a given host, in this case, the local machine, as follows:

```
$ python 7_3_print_remote_cpu_info.py
Enter the username:faruq
Enter password for faruq:
exit status:  0
processor     : 0
vendor_id     : GenuineIntel
cpu family     : 6
model         : 42
model name     : Intel(R) Core(TM) i5-2400S CPU @ 2.50GHz
stepping     : 7
cpu MHz          : 2469.677
cache size     : 6144 KB
fdiv_bug     : no
hlt_bug          : no
f00f_bug     : no
coma_bug     : no
fpu          : yes
fpu_exception     : yes
cpuid level     : 5
wp          : yes
flags          : fpu vme de pse tsc msr pae mce cx8 apic sep mtrr pge mca
cmov pat pse36 clflush mmx fxsr sse sse2 syscall nx rdtscp lm constant_
tsc up pni monitor ssse3 lahf_lm
bogomips     : 4939.35
clflush size     : 64
cache_alignment     : 64
address sizes     : 36 bits physical, 48 bits virtual
power management:
```

How it works...

First, we collect the connection parameters such as hostname, port, username, and password. These parameters are then passed to the `print_remote_cpu_info()` function.

This function creates an SSH client session by calling the `transport` class of `paramiko`. The connection is made thereafter using the supplied username and password. We can create a raw communication session using `open_channel()` on the SSH client. In order to execute a command on the remote host, `exec_command()` can be used.

After sending the command to the remote host, the response from the remote host can be caught by blocking the `recv_ready()` event of the session object. We can create two lists, `stdout_data` and `stderr_data`, and use them to store the remote output and error messages.

When the command exits in the remote machine, it can be detected using the `exit_status_ready()` method, and the remote session data can be concatenated using the `join()` string method.

Finally, the session and client connection can be closed using the `close()` method on each object.

Installing a Python package remotely

While dealing with the remote host in the previous recipes, you may have noticed that we need to do a lot of stuff related to the connection setup. For efficient execution, it is desirable that they become abstract and only the relevant high-level part is exposed to the programmers. It is cumbersome and slow to always explicitly set up connections to execute commands remotely.

Fabric (`http://fabfile.org/`), a third-party Python module, solves this problem. It only exposes as many APIs as can be used to efficiently interact with remote machines.

In this recipe, a simple example of using Fabric will be shown.

Getting ready

We need Fabric to be installed first. You can install Fabric using the Python packing tools, `pip` or `easy_install`, as shown in the following command. Fabric relies on the `paramiko` module, which will be installed automatically.

```
$ pip install fabric
```

Here, we will connect the remote host using the SSH protocol. So, it's necessary to run the SSH server on the remote end. If you like to test with your local machine (pretending to access as a remote machine), you may install the `openssh` server package locally. On a Debian/Ubuntu machine, this can be done with the package manager, `apt-get`, as shown in the following command:

```
$ sudo apt-get install openssh-server
```

How to do it...

Here's the code for installing a Python package using Fabric.

Listing 7.4 gives the code for installing a Python package remotely as follows:

```
#!/usr/bin/env python
# Python Network Programming Cookbook -- Chapter - 7
# This program is optimized for Python 2.7.
# It may run on any other version with/without modifications.

from getpass import getpass
from fabric.api import settings, run, env, prompt

def remote_server():
  env.hosts = ['127.0.0.1']
  env.user = prompt('Enter user name: ')
  env.password = getpass('Enter password: ')

def install_package():
  run("pip install yolk")
```

Fabric scripts are run in a different way as compared to the normal Python scripts. All functions using the `fabric` library must be referred to a Python script called `fabfile.py`. There's no traditional `__main__` directive in this script. Instead, you can define your method using the Fabric APIs and execute these methods using the command-line tool, `fab`. So, instead of calling `python <script>.py`, you can run a Fabric script, which is defined in a `fabfile.py` script and located under the current directory, by calling `fab one_function_name another_function_name`.

So, let's create a `fabfile.py` script as shown in the following command. For the sake of simplicity, you can create a file shortcut or link from any file to a `fabfile.py` script. First, delete any previously created `fabfile.py` file and create a shortcut to `fabfile`:

```
$ rm -rf fabfile.py
$ ln -s 7_4_install_python_package_remotely.py fabfile.py
```

If you call the fabfile now, it will produce the following output after installing the Python package, `yolk`, remotely as follows:

```
$ ln -sfn 7_4_install_python_package_remotely.py fabfile.py
$ fab remote_server install_package
Enter user name: faruq
Enter password:
[127.0.0.1] Executing task 'install_package'
[127.0.0.1] run: pip install yolk
[127.0.0.1] out: Downloading/unpacking yolk
[127.0.0.1] out:   Downloading yolk-0.4.3.tar.gz (86kB):
[127.0.0.1] out:   Downloading yolk-0.4.3.tar.gz (86kB): 100%  86kB
[127.0.0.1] out:   Downloading yolk-0.4.3.tar.gz (86kB):
[127.0.0.1] out:   Downloading yolk-0.4.3.tar.gz (86kB): 86kB
downloaded
[127.0.0.1] out:   Running setup.py egg_info for package yolk
[127.0.0.1] out:     Installing yolk script to /home/faruq/env/bin
[127.0.0.1] out: Successfully installed yolk
[127.0.0.1] out: Cleaning up...
[127.0.0.1] out:


Done.
Disconnecting from 127.0.0.1... done.
```

How it works...

This recipe demonstrates how a system administration task can be done remotely using a Python script. There are two functions present in this script. The `remote_server()` function sets up the Fabric `env` environment variables, for example, the hostname, user, password, and so on.

The other function, `install_package()`, calls the `run()` function. This takes the commands that you usually type in the command line. In this case, the command is `pip install yolk`. This installs the Python package, `yolk`, with `pip`. As compared to the previously described recipes, this method of running a remote command using Fabric is easier and more efficient.

Running a MySQL command remotely

If you ever need to administer a MySQL server remotely, this recipe is for you. It will show you how to send database commands to a remote MySQL server from a Python script. If you need to set up a web application that relies on a backend database, this recipe can be used as a part of your web application setup process.

Getting ready

This recipe also needs Fabric to be installed first. You can install Fabric using the Python packing tools, `pip` or `easy_install`, as shown in the following command. Fabric relies on the `paramiko` module, which will be installed automatically.

```
$ pip install fabric
```

Here, we will connect the remote host using the SSH protocol. So, it's necessary to run the SSH server on the remote end. You also need to run a MySQL server on the remote host. On a Debian/Ubuntu machine, this can be done with the package manager, `apt-get`, as shown in the following command:

```
$ sudo apt-get install openssh-server mysql-server
```

How to do it...

We defined the Fabric environment settings and a few functions for administering MySQL remotely. In these functions, instead of calling the `mysql` executable directly, we send the SQL commands to `mysql` via `echo`. This ensures that arguments are passed properly to the `mysql` executable.

Listing 7.5 gives the code for running MySQL commands remotely, as follows:

```
#!/usr/bin/env python
# Python Network Programming Cookbook -- Chapter - 7
# This program is optimized for Python 2.7.
# It may run on any other version with/without modifications.

from getpass import getpass
from fabric.api import run, env, prompt, cd

def remote_server():
  env.hosts = ['127.0.0.1']
# Edit this list to include remote hosts
  env.user =prompt('Enter your system username: ')
  env.password = getpass('Enter your system user password: ')
  env.mysqlhost = 'localhost'
  env.mysqluser = 'root'prompt('Enter your db username: ')
```

```
  env.password = getpass('Enter your db user password: ')
  env.db_name = ''

def show_dbs():
  """ Wraps mysql show databases cmd"""
  q = "show databases"
  run("echo '%s' | mysql -u%s -p%s" %(q, env.mysqluser,
env.mysqlpassword))


def run_sql(db_name, query):
  """ Generic function to run sql"""
  with cd('/tmp'):
    run("echo '%s' | mysql -u%s -p%s -D %s" %(query,
env.mysqluser, env.mysqlpassword, db_name))

def create_db():
  """Create a MySQL DB for App version"""
  if not env.db_name:
    db_name = prompt("Enter the DB name:")
  else:
    db_name = env.db_name
  run('echo "CREATE DATABASE %s default character set utf8 collate
utf8_unicode_ci;"|mysql --batch --user=%s --password=%s --
host=%s'\
    % (db_name, env.mysqluser, env.mysqlpassword, env.mysqlhost),
pty=True)

def ls_db():
  """ List a dbs with size in MB """
  if not env.db_name:
    db_name = prompt("Which DB to ls?")
  else:
    db_name = env.db_name
  query = """SELECT table_schema
"DB Name",
  Round(Sum(data_length + index_length) / 1024 / 1024, 1) "DB Size
in MB"
    FROM   information_schema.tables
    WHERE table_schema = \"%s\"
    GROUP  BY table_schema """ %db_name
  run_sql(db_name, query)
```

```
def empty_db():
  """ Empty all tables of a given DB """
  db_name = prompt("Enter DB name to empty:")
  cmd = """
  (echo 'SET foreign_key_checks = 0;';
  (mysqldump -u%s -p%s --add-drop-table --no-data %s |
  grep ^DROP);
  echo 'SET foreign_key_checks = 1;') | \
  mysql -u%s -p%s -b %s
  """ %(env.mysqluser, env.mysqlpassword, db_name, env.mysqluser,
env.mysqlpassword, db_name)
  run(cmd)
```

In order to run this script, you should create a shortcut, `fabfile.py`. From the command line, you can do this by typing the following command:

```
$ ln -sfn 7_5_run_mysql_command_remotely.py fabfile.py
```

Then, you can call the `fab` executable in various forms.

The following command will show a list of databases (using the SQL query, `show databases`):

```
$ fab remote_server show_dbs
```

The following command will create a new MySQL database. If you haven't defined the Fabric environment variable, `db_name`, a prompt will be shown to enter the target database name. This database will be created using the SQL command, `CREATE DATABASE <database_name> default character set utf8 collate utf8_unicode_ci;`.

```
$ fab remote_server create_db
```

This Fabric command will show the size of a database:

```
$ fab remote_server ls_db()
```

The following Fabric command will use the `mysqldump` and `mysql` executables to empty a database. This behavior of this function is similar to the truncating of a database, except it removes all the tables. The result is as if you created a fresh database without any tables:

```
$ fab remote_server empty_db()
```

The following will be the output:

```
$ $ fab remote_server show_dbs
[127.0.0.1] Executing task 'show_dbs'
[127.0.0.1] run: echo 'show databases' | mysql -uroot -p<DELETED>
[127.0.0.1] out: Database
```

```
[127.0.0.1] out: information_schema
[127.0.0.1] out: mysql
[127.0.0.1] out: phpmyadmin
[127.0.0.1] out:


Done.
Disconnecting from 127.0.0.1... done.


$ fab remote_server create_db
[127.0.0.1] Executing task 'create_db'
Enter the DB name: test123
[127.0.0.1] run: echo "CREATE DATABASE test123 default character set utf8
collate utf8_unicode_ci;"|mysql --batch --user=root --password=<DELETED>
--host=localhost

Done.
Disconnecting from 127.0.0.1... done.
$ fab remote_server show_dbs
[127.0.0.1] Executing task 'show_dbs'
[127.0.0.1] run: echo 'show databases' | mysql -uroot -p<DELETED>
[127.0.0.1] out: Database
[127.0.0.1] out: information_schema
[127.0.0.1] out: collabtive
[127.0.0.1] out: test123
[127.0.0.1] out: testdb
[127.0.0.1] out:

Done.
Disconnecting from 127.0.0.1... done.
```

How it works...

This script defines a few functions that are used with Fabric. The first function, `remote_server()`, sets the environment variables. The local loopback IP (`127.0.0.1`) is put to the list of hosts. The local system user and MySQL login credentials are set and collected via `getpass()`.

The other function utilizes the Fabric `run()` function to send MySQL commands to the remote MySQL server by echoing the command to the `mysql` executable.

The `run_sql()` function is a generic function that can be used as a wrapper in other functions. For example, the `empty_db()` function calls it to execute the SQL commands. This can keep your code a bit more organized and cleaner.

Transferring files to a remote machine over SSH

While automating a remote system administration task using Fabric, if you want to transfer files between your local machine and the remote machine with SSH, you can use the Fabric's built-in `get()` and `put()` functions. This recipe shows you how we can create custom functions to transfer files smartly by checking the disk space before and after the transfer.

Getting ready

This recipe also needs Fabric to be installed first. You can install Fabric using Python packing tools, `pip` or `easy_install`, as shown in the following command:

```
$ pip install fabric
```

Here, we will connect the remote host using the SSH protocol. So, it's necessary to install and run the SSH server on the remote host.

How to do it...

Let us first set up the Fabric environment variables and then create two functions, one for downloading files and the other for uploading files.

Listing 7.6 gives the code for transferring files to a remote machine over SSH as follows:

```
#!/usr/bin/env python
# Python Network Programming Cookbook -- Chapter - 7
# This program is optimized for Python 2.7.
# It may run on any other version with/without modifications.

from getpass import getpass
from fabric.api import local, run, env, get, put, prompt, open_shell

def remote_server():
  env.hosts = ['127.0.0.1']
  env.password = getpass('Enter your system password: ')
  env.home_folder = '/tmp'

def login():
```

```
    open_shell(command="cd %s" %env.home_folder)


def download_file():
    print "Checking local disk space..."
    local("df -h")
    remote_path = prompt("Enter the remote file path:")
    local_path = prompt("Enter the local file path:")
    get(remote_path=remote_path, local_path=local_path)
    local("ls %s" %local_path)


def upload_file():
    print "Checking remote disk space..."
    run("df -h")
    local_path = prompt("Enter the local file path:")
    remote_path = prompt("Enter the remote file path:")
    put(remote_path=remote_path, local_path=local_path)
    run("ls %s" %remote_path)
```

In order to run this script, you should create a shortcut, `fabfile.py`. From the command line, you can do this by typing the following command:

```
$ ln -sfn 7_6_transfer_file_over_ssh.py fabfile.py
```

Then, you can call the `fab` executable in various forms.

First, to log on to a remote server using your script, you can run the following Fabric function:

```
$ fab remote_server login
```

This will give you a minimum shell-like environment. Then, you can download a file from a remote server to your local machine using the following command:

```
$ fab remote_server download_file
```

Similarly, to upload a file, you can use the following command:

```
$ fab remote_server upload_file
```

In this example, the local machine is used via SSH. So, you have to install the SSH server locally to run these scripts. Otherwise, you can modify the `remote_server()` function and point it to a remote server, as follows:

```
$ fab remote_server login
[127.0.0.1] Executing task 'login'
Linux debian6 2.6.32-5-686 #1 SMP Mon Feb 25 01:04:36 UTC 2013 i686


The programs included with the Debian GNU/Linux system are free software;
```

```
the exact distribution terms for each program are described in the
individual files in /usr/share/doc/*/copyright.

Debian GNU/Linux comes with ABSOLUTELY NO WARRANTY, to the extent
permitted by applicable law.
You have new mail.
Last login: Wed Aug 21 15:08:45 2013 from localhost
cd /tmp
faruq@debian6:~$ cd /tmp
faruq@debian6:/tmp$

<CTRL+D>
faruq@debian6:/tmp$ logout

Done.
Disconnecting from 127.0.0.1... done.

$ fab remote_server download_file
[127.0.0.1] Executing task 'download_file'
Checking local disk space...
[localhost] local: df -h
Filesystem            Size  Used Avail Use% Mounted on
/dev/sda1              62G   47G   12G  81% /
tmpfs                 506M     0  506M   0% /lib/init/rw
udev                  501M  160K  501M   1% /dev
tmpfs                 506M  408K  505M   1% /dev/shm
Z_DRIVE              1012G  944G   69G  94% /media/z
C_DRIVE               466G  248G  218G  54% /media/c
Enter the remote file path: /tmp/op.txt
Enter the local file path: .
[127.0.0.1] download: chapter7/op.txt <- /tmp/op.txt
[localhost] local: ls .
7_1_execute_remote_telnet_cmd.py   7_3_print_remote_cpu_info.py
7_5_run_mysql_command_remotely.py  7_7_configure_Apache_for_hosting_
website_remotely.py  fabfile.pyc  __init__.py  test.txt
7_2_copy_remote_file_over_sftp.py  7_4_install_python_package_
remotely.py  7_6_transfer_file_over_ssh.py      fabfile.py
index.html     op.txt       vhost.conf

Done.
Disconnecting from 127.0.0.1... done.
```

How it works...

In this recipe, we used a few of Fabric's built-in functions to transfer files between local and remote machines. The `local()` function does an action on the local machine, whereas the remote actions are carried out by the `run()` function.

This is useful to check the available disk space on the target machine before uploading a file and vice versa.

This is achieved by using the Unix command, `df`. The source and destination file paths can be specified via the command prompt or can be hard coded in the source file in case of an unattended automatic execution.

Configuring Apache remotely to host a website

Fabric functions can be run as both regular and super users. If you need to host a website in a remote Apache web server, you need the administrative user privileges to create configuration files and restart the web server. This recipe introduces the Fabric `sudo()` function that runs commands in the remote machine as a superuser. Here, we would like to configure the Apache virtual host for running a website.

Getting ready

This recipe needs Fabric to be installed first on your local machine. You can install Fabric using the Python packing tools, `pip` or `easy_install`, as shown in the following command:

```
$ pip install fabric
```

Here, we will connect the remote host using the SSH protocol. So, it's necessary to install and run the SSH server on the remote host. It is also assumed that the Apache web server is installed and running on the remote server. On a Debian/Ubuntu machine, this can be done with the package manager, `apt-get`, as shown in the following command:

```
$ sudo apt-get install openssh-server apache2
```

How to do it...

First, we collect our Apache installation paths and some configuration parameters, such as web server user, group, virtual host configuration path, and initialization scripts. These parameters can be defined as constants.

Then, we set up two functions, `remote_server()` and `setup_vhost()`, to execute the Apache configuration task using Fabric.

Listing 7.7 gives the code for configuring Apache remotely to host a website as follows:

```
#!/usr/bin/env python
# Python Network Programming Cookbook -- Chapter - 7
# This program is optimized for Python 2.7.
# It may run on any other version with/without modifications.

from fabric.api import env, put, sudo, prompt
from fabric.contrib.files import exists

WWW_DOC_ROOT = "/data/apache/test/"
WWW_USER = "www-data"
WWW_GROUP = "www-data"
APACHE_SITES_PATH = "/etc/apache2/sites-enabled/"
APACHE_INIT_SCRIPT = "/etc/init.d/apache2 "

def remote_server():
  env.hosts = ['127.0.0.1']
  env.user = prompt('Enter user name: ')
  env.password = getpass('Enter your system password: ')


def setup_vhost():
  """ Setup a test website """
  print "Preparing the Apache vhost setup..."

  print "Setting up the document root..."
  if exists(WWW_DOC_ROOT):
    sudo("rm -rf %s" %WWW_DOC_ROOT)
  sudo("mkdir -p %s" %WWW_DOC_ROOT)

  # setup file permissions
  sudo("chown -R %s.%s %s" %(env.user, env.user, WWW_DOC_ROOT))

  # upload a sample index.html file
  put(local_path="index.html", remote_path=WWW_DOC_ROOT)
  sudo("chown -R %s.%s %s" %(WWW_USER, WWW_GROUP, WWW_DOC_ROOT))

  print "Setting up the vhost..."
  sudo("chown -R %s.%s %s" %(env.user, env.user,
APACHE_SITES_PATH))
```

```
    # upload a pre-configured vhost.conf
    put(local_path="vhost.conf", remote_path=APACHE_SITES_PATH)
    sudo("chown -R %s.%s %s" %('root', 'root', APACHE_SITES_PATH))

    # restart Apache to take effect
    sudo("%s restart" %APACHE_INIT_SCRIPT)
    print "Setup complete. Now open the server path
http://abc.remote-server.org/ in your web browser."
```

In order to run this script, the following line should be appended on your host file, for example,. `/etc/hosts`:

```
127.0.0.1 abc.remote-server.org abc
```

You should also create a shortcut, `fabfile.py`. From the command line, you can do this by typing the following command:

```
$ ln -sfn 7_7_configure_Apache_for_hosting_website_remotely.py
fabfile.py
```

Then, you can call the `fab` executable in various forms.

First, to log on to a remote server using your script, you can run the following Fabric function. This will result in the following output:

```
$ fab remote_server setup_vhost
[127.0.0.1] Executing task 'setup_vhost'
Preparing the Apache vhost setup...
Setting up the document root...
[127.0.0.1] sudo: rm -rf /data/apache/test/
[127.0.0.1] sudo: mkdir -p /data/apache/test/
[127.0.0.1] sudo: chown -R faruq.faruq /data/apache/test/
[127.0.0.1] put: index.html -> /data/apache/test/index.html
[127.0.0.1] sudo: chown -R www-data.www-data /data/apache/test/
Setting up the vhost...
[127.0.0.1] sudo: chown -R faruq.faruq /etc/apache2/sites-enabled/
[127.0.0.1] put: vhost.conf -> /etc/apache2/sites-enabled/vhost.conf
[127.0.0.1] sudo: chown -R root.root /etc/apache2/sites-enabled/
[127.0.0.1] sudo: /etc/init.d/apache2 restart
[127.0.0.1] out: Restarting web server: apache2apache2: Could not
reliably determine the server's fully qualified domain name, using
127.0.0.1 for ServerName
```

```
[127.0.0.1] out:  ... waiting apache2: Could not reliably determine the
server's fully qualified domain name, using 127.0.0.1 for ServerName
[127.0.0.1] out: .
[127.0.0.1] out:


Setup complete. Now open the server path http://abc.remote-server.org/ in
your web browser.


Done.
Disconnecting from 127.0.0.1... done.
```

After you run this recipe, you can open your browser and try to access the path you set up on the host file (for example, `/etc/hosts`). It should show the following output on your browser:

```
It works!
This is the default web page for this server.
The web server software is running but no content has been added,

yet.
```

How it works...

This recipe sets up the initial Apache configuration parameters as constants and then defines two functions. In the `remote_server()` function, the usual Fabric environment parameters, for example, hosts, user, password, and so on, are placed.

The `setup_vhost()` function executes a series of privileged commands. First, it checks whether the website's document root path is already created using the `exists()` function. If it exists, it removes that path and creates it in the next step. Using `chown`, it ensures that the path is owned by the current user.

In the next step, it uploads a bare bone HTML file, `index.html`, to the document root path. After uploading the file, it reverts the permission of the files to the web server user.

After setting up the document root, the `setup_vhost()` function uploads the supplied `vhost.conf` file to the Apache site configuration path. Then, it sets its owner as the root user.

Finally, the script restarts the Apache service so that the configuration is activated. If the configuration is successful, you should see the sample output shown earlier when you open the URL, `http://abc.remote-server.org/`, in your browser.

8

Working with Web Services – XML-RPC, SOAP, and REST

In this chapter, we will cover the following recipes:

- Querying a local XML-RPC server
- Writing a multithreaded, multicall XML-RPC server
- Running an XML-RPC server with a basic HTTP authentication
- Collecting some photo information from Flickr using REST
- Searching for SOAP methods from an Amazon S3 web service
- Searching Google for custom information
- Searching Amazon for books through product search API

Introduction

This chapter presents some interesting Python recipes on web services using three different approaches, namely, **XML Remote Procedure Call** (**XML-RPC**), **Simple Object Access Protocol** (**SOAP**), and **Representational State Transfer** (**REST**). The idea behind the web services is to enable an interaction between two software components over the Web through a carefully designed protocol. The interface is machine readable. Various protocols are used to facilitate the web services.

Here, we bring examples from three commonly used protocols. XML-RPC uses HTTP as the transport medium, and communication is done using XML contents. A server that implements XML-RPC waits for a call from a suitable client. The client calls that server to execute remote procedures with different parameters. XML-RPC is simpler and comes with a minimum security in mind. On the other hand, SOAP has a rich set of protocols for enhanced remote procedure calls. REST is an architectural style to facilitate web services. It operates with HTTP request methods, namely, `GET`, `POST`, `PUT`, and `DELETE`. This chapter presents the practical use of these web services protocols and styles to achieve some common tasks.

Querying a local XML-RPC server

If you do a lot of web programming, it's most likely that you will come across this task: to get some information from a website that runs an XML-RPC service. Before we go into the depth of an XML-RPC service, let's launch an XML-RPC server and talk to it first.

Getting ready

In this recipe, we will use the Python Supervisor program that is widely used to launch and manage a bunch of executable programs. Supervisor can be run as a background daemon and can monitor child processes and restart if they die suddenly. We can install Supervisor by simply running the following command:

```
$pip install supervisor
```

How to do it...

We need to create a configuration file for Supervisor. A sample configuration is given in this recipe. In this example, we define the Unix HTTP server socket and a few other parameters. Note the `rpcinterface:supervisor` section where `rpcinterface_factory` is defined to communicate with clients.

Using Supervisor, we configure a simple server program in the `program:8_2_multithreaded_multicall_xmlrpc_server.py` section by specifying the command and some other parameters.

Listing 8.1a gives the code for a minimal Supervisor configuration, as shown:

```
[unix_http_server]
file=/tmp/supervisor.sock   ; (the path to the socket file)
chmod=0700                 ; socket file mode (default 0700)

[supervisord]
logfile=/tmp/supervisord.log
loglevel=info
```

```
pidfile=/tmp/supervisord.pid
nodaemon=true

[rpcinterface:supervisor]
supervisor.rpcinterface_factory = supervisor.rpcinterface:make_main_
rpcinterface

[program:8_2_multithreaded_multicall_xmlrpc_server.py]
command=python 8_2_multithreaded_multicall_xmlrpc_server.py ; the
program (relative uses PATH, can take args)
process_name=%(program_name)s ; process_name expr (default
%(program_name)s)
```

If you create the preceding Supervisor configuration file in your favorite editor, you can run Supervisor by simply calling it.

Now, we can code an XML-RPC client that can act as a Supervisor proxy and give us the information about the running processes.

Listing 8.1b gives the code for querying a local XML-RPC server, as shown:

```
#!/usr/bin/env python
# Python Network Programming Cookbook -- Chapter - 8
# This program is optimized for Python 2.7.
# It may run on any other version with/without modifications.
import supervisor.xmlrpc
import xmlrpclib

def query_supervisr(sock):
    transport = supervisor.xmlrpc.SupervisorTransport(None, None,
                'unix://%s' %sock)
    proxy = xmlrpclib.ServerProxy('http://127.0.0.1',
            transport=transport)
    print "Getting info about all running processes via
Supervisord..."
    print proxy.supervisor.getAllProcessInfo()

if __name__ == '__main__':
    query_supervisr(sock='/tmp/supervisor.sock')
```

If you run the Supervisor daemon, it will show the output similar to the following:

```
chapter8$ supervisord
2013-09-27 16:40:56,861 INFO RPC interface 'supervisor' initialized
2013-09-27 16:40:56,861 CRIT Server 'unix_http_server' running
without any HTTP authentication checking
```

```
2013-09-27 16:40:56,861 INFO supervisord started with pid 27436
2013-09-27 16:40:57,864 INFO spawned:
'8_2_multithreaded_multicall_xmlrpc_server.py' with pid 27439
2013-09-27 16:40:58,940 INFO success:
8_2_multithreaded_multicall_xmlrpc_server.py entered RUNNING state,
process has stayed up for > than 1 seconds (startsecs)
```

Note that our child process, `8_2_multithreaded_multicall_xmlrpc_server.py`, has been launched.

Now, if you run the client code, it will query the XML-RPC server interface of Supervisor and list the running processes, as shown:

```
$ python 8_1_query_xmlrpc_server.py
Getting info about all running processes via Supervisord...
[{'now': 1380296807, 'group':
'8_2_multithreaded_multicall_xmlrpc_server.py', 'description': 'pid
27439, uptime 0:05:50', 'pid': 27439, 'stderr_logfile':
'/tmp/8_2_multithreaded_multicall_xmlrpc_server.py-stderr---
supervisor-i_VmKz.log', 'stop': 0, 'statename': 'RUNNING', 'start':
1380296457, 'state': 20, 'stdout_logfile':
'/tmp/8_2_multithreaded_multicall_xmlrpc_server.py-stdout---
supervisor-eMuJqk.log', 'logfile':
'/tmp/8_2_multithreaded_multicall_xmlrpc_server.py-stdout---
supervisor-eMuJqk.log', 'exitstatus': 0, 'spawnerr': '', 'name':
'8_2_multithreaded_multicall_xmlrpc_server.py'}]
```

How it works...

This recipe relies on running the Supervisor daemon (configured with `rpcinterface`) in the background. Supervisor launches another XML-RPC server, as follows: `8_2_multithreaded_multicall_xmlrpc_server.py`.

The client code has a `query_supervisr()` method, which takes an argument for the Supervisor socket. In this method, an instance of `SupervisorTransport` is created with the Unix socket path. Then, an XML-RPC server proxy is created by instantiating the `ServerProxy()` class of `xmlrpclib` by passing the server address and previously created `transport`.

The XML-RPC server proxy then calls the Supervisor's `getAllProcessInfo()` method, which prints the process information of the child process. This process includes `pid`, `statename`, `description`, and so on.

Writing a multithreaded multicall XML-RPC server

You can make your XML-RPC server accept multiple calls simultaneously. This means that multiple function calls can return a single result. In addition to this, if your server is multithreaded, then you can execute more code after the server is launched in a single thread. The program's main thread will not be blocked in this manner.

How to do it...

We can create a `ServerThread` class inheriting from the `threading.Thread` class and wrap a `SimpleXMLRPCServer` instance in an attribute of this class. This can be set up to accept multiple calls.

Then, we can create two functions: one launches the multithreaded, multicall XML-RPC server and the other creates a client to that server.

Listing 8.2 gives the code for writing a multithreaded, multicall XML-RPC server, as shown:

```
#!/usr/bin/env python
# Python Network Programming Cookbook -- Chapter - 8
# This program is optimized for Python 2.7.
# It may run on any other version with/without modifications.

import argparse
import xmlrpclib
import threading

from SimpleXMLRPCServer import SimpleXMLRPCServer

# some trivial functions
def add(x,y):
  return x+y

def subtract(x, y):
  return x-y

def multiply(x, y):
  return x*y

def divide(x, y):
  return x/y
```

```
class ServerThread(threading.Thread):
  def __init__(self, server_addr):
    threading.Thread.__init__(self)
    self.server = SimpleXMLRPCServer(server_addr)
    self.server.register_multicall_functions()
    self.server.register_function(add, 'add')
    self.server.register_function(subtract, 'subtract')
    self.server.register_function(multiply, 'multiply')
    self.server.register_function(divide, 'divide')

  def run(self):
    self.server.serve_forever()

def run_server(host, port):
  # server code
  server_addr = (host, port)
  server = ServerThread(server_addr)
  server.start() # The server is now running
  print "Server thread started. Testing the server..."

def run_client(host, port):
  # client code
  proxy = xmlrpclib.ServerProxy("http://%s:%s/" %(host, port))
  multicall = xmlrpclib.MultiCall(proxy)
  multicall.add(7,3)
  multicall.subtract(7,3)
  multicall.multiply(7,3)
  multicall.divide(7,3)
  result = multicall()
  print "7+3=%d, 7-3=%d, 7*3=%d, 7/3=%d" % tuple(result)

if __name__ == '__main__':
  parser = argparse.ArgumentParser(description='Multithreaded
multicall XMLRPC Server/Proxy')
  parser.add_argument('--host', action="store", dest="host",
default='localhost')
  parser.add_argument('--port', action="store", dest="port",
default=8000, type=int)
  # parse arguments
  given_args = parser.parse_args()
  host, port =  given_args.host, given_args.port
  run_server(host, port)
  run_client(host, port)
```

If you run this script, you will see the output similar to the following:

```
$ python 8_2_multithreaded_multicall_xmlrpc_server.py --port=8000
Server thread started. Testing the server...
localhost - - [25/Sep/2013 17:38:32] "POST / HTTP/1.1" 200 -
7+3=10, 7-3=4, 7*3=21, 7/3=2
```

How it works...

In this recipe, we have created a `ServerThread` subclass inheriting from the Python threading library's `Thread` class. This subclass initializes a server attribute that creates an instance of the `SimpleXMLRPC` server. The XML-RPC server address can be given via the command-line input. In order to enable the multicall function, we called the `register_multicall_functions()` method on the server instance.

Then, four trivial functions are registered with this XML-RPC server: `add()`, `subtract()`, `multiply()`, and `divide()`. These functions do exactly the same operation as their names suggest.

In order to launch the server, we pass a host and port to the `run_server()` function. A server instance is created using the `ServerThread` class discussed earlier. The `start()` method of this server instance launches the XML-RPC server.

On the client side, the `run_client()` function accepts the same host and port arguments from the command line. It then creates a proxy instance of the XML-RPC server discussed earlier by calling the `ServerProxy()` class from `xmlrpclib`. This proxy instance is then passed onto the `MultiCall` class instance, `multicall`. Now, the preceding four trivial RPC methods can be run, for example, `add`, `subtract`, `multiply`, and `divide`. Finally, we can get the result via a single call, for example, `multicall()`. The result tuple is then printed in a single line.

Running an XML-RPC server with a basic HTTP authentication

Sometimes, you may need to implement authentication with an XML-RPC server. This recipe presents an example of a basic HTTP authentication with an XML-RPC server.

How to do it...

We can create a subclass of `SimpleXMLRPCServer` and override its request handler so that when a request comes, it is verified against a given login credentials.

Listing 8.3a gives the code for running an XML-RPC server with a basic HTTP authentication, as shown:

```
#!/usr/bin/env python
# Python Network Programming Cookbook -- Chapter - 8
# This program is optimized for Python 2.7.
# It may run on any other version with/without modifications.

import argparse
import xmlrpclib
from base64 import b64decode
from SimpleXMLRPCServer  import SimpleXMLRPCServer,
SimpleXMLRPCRequestHandler


class SecureXMLRPCServer(SimpleXMLRPCServer):

  def __init__(self, host, port, username, password, *args,
**kargs):
    self.username = username
    self.password = password
    # authenticate method is called from inner class
    class VerifyingRequestHandler(SimpleXMLRPCRequestHandler):
      # method to override
      def parse_request(request):
        if\ SimpleXMLRPCRequestHandler.parse_request(request):
        # authenticate
          if self.authenticate(request.headers):
        return True
          else:
            # if authentication fails return 401
              request.send_error(401, 'Authentication\ failed
ZZZ')
            return False
          # initialize
         SimpleXMLRPCServer.__init__(self, (host, port),
requestHandler=VerifyingRequestHandler, *args, **kargs)

  def authenticate(self, headers):
    headers = headers.get('Authorization').split()
    basic, encoded = headers[0], headers[1]
    if basic != 'Basic':
      print 'Only basic authentication supported'
    return False
    secret = b64decode(encoded).split(':')
```

```
        username, password = secret[0], secret[1]
      return True if (username == self.username and password ==
self.password) else False


def run_server(host, port, username, password):
  server = SecureXMLRPCServer(host, port, username, password)
  # simple test function
  def echo(msg):
    """Reply client in  upper case """
    reply = msg.upper()
    print "Client said: %s. So we echo that in uppercase: %s"
%(msg, reply)
    return reply
  server.register_function(echo, 'echo')
  print "Running a HTTP auth enabled XMLRPC server on %s:%s..."
%(host, port)
  server.serve_forever()


if __name__ == '__main__':
  parser = argparse.ArgumentParser(description='Multithreaded
multicall XMLRPC Server/Proxy')
  parser.add_argument('--host', action="store", dest="host",
default='localhost')
  parser.add_argument('--port', action="store", dest="port",
default=8000, type=int)
  parser.add_argument('--username', action="store",
dest="username", default='user')
  parser.add_argument('--password', action="store",
dest="password", default='pass')
  # parse arguments
  given_args = parser.parse_args()
  host, port =  given_args.host, given_args.port
  username, password = given_args.username, given_args.password
  run_server(host, port, username, password)
```

If this server is run, then the following output can be seen by default:

```
$ python 8_3a_xmlrpc_server_with_http_auth.py
Running a HTTP auth enabled XMLRPC server on localhost:8000...
Client said: hello server.... So we echo that in uppercase: HELLO
SERVER...
localhost - - [27/Sep/2013 12:08:57] "POST /RPC2 HTTP/1.1" 200 -
```

Now, let us create a simple client proxy and use the same login credentials as used with the server.

Listing 8.3b gives the code for the XML-RPC Client, as shown:

```
#!/usr/bin/env python
# Python Network Programming Cookbook -- Chapter - 8
# This program is optimized for Python 2.7.
# It may run on any other version with/without modifications.

import argparse
import xmlrpclib

def run_client(host, port, username, password):
  server = xmlrpclib.ServerProxy('http://%s:%s@%s:%s' %(username,
password, host, port, ))
  msg = "hello server..."
  print "Sending message to server: %s  " %msg
  print "Got reply: %s" %server.echo(msg)

if __name__ == '__main__':
  parser = argparse.ArgumentParser(description='Multithreaded
multicall XMLRPC Server/Proxy')
  parser.add_argument('--host', action="store", dest="host",
default='localhost')
  parser.add_argument('--port', action="store", dest="port",
default=8000, type=int)
  parser.add_argument('--username', action="store",
dest="username", default='user')
  parser.add_argument('--password', action="store",
dest="password", default='pass')
  # parse arguments
  given_args = parser.parse_args()
  host, port =  given_args.host, given_args.port
  username, password = given_args.username, given_args.password
  run_client(host, port, username, password)
```

If you run the client, then it shows the following output:

```
$ python 8_3b_xmprpc_client.py
Sending message to server: hello server...
Got reply: HELLO SERVER...
```

How it works...

In the server script, the `SecureXMLRPCServer` subclass is created by inheriting from `SimpleXMLRPCServer`. In this subclass' initialization code, we created the `VerifyingRequestHandler` class that actually intercepts the request and does the basic authentication using the `authenticate()` method.

In the `authenticate()` method, the HTTP request is passed as an argument. This method checks the presence of the value of `Authorization`. If its value is set to `Basic`, it then decodes the encoded password with the `b64decode()` function from the `base64` standard module. After extracting the username and password, it then checks that with the server's given credentials set up initially.

In the `run_server()` function, a simple `echo()` subfunction is defined and registered with the `SecureXMLRPCServer` instance.

In the client script, `run_client()` simply takes the server address and login credentials and passes them to the `ServerProxy()` instance. It then sends a single line message via the `echo()` method.

Collecting some photo information from Flickr using REST

Many Internet websites provide a web services interface through their REST APIs. **Flickr**, a famous photo sharing website, has a REST interface. Let's try to gather some photo information to build a specialized database or other photo-related application.

How to do it...

We need the REST URLs for making the HTTP requests. For simplicity's sake, the URLs are hard coded in this recipe. We can use the third-party `requests` module to make the REST requests. It has the convenient `get()`, `post()`, `put()`, and `delete()` methods.

In order to talk to Flickr web services, you need to register yourself and get a secret API key. This API key can be placed in a `local_settings.py` file or supplied via the command line.

Listing 8.4 gives the code for collecting some photo information from Flickr using REST, as shown:

```
#!/usr/bin/env python
# Python Network Programming Cookbook -- Chapter - 8
# This program is optimized for Python 2.7.
# It may run on any other version with/without modifications.
```

```
import argparse
import json
import requests

try:
    from local_settings import flickr_apikey
except ImportError:
    pass

def collect_photo_info(api_key, tag, max_count):
    """Collects some interesting info about some photos from Flickr.
com for a given tag """
    photo_collection = []
    url =  "http://api.flickr.com/services/rest/?method=flickr.photos.
search&tags=%s&format=json&nojsoncallback=1&api_key=%s" %(tag, api_
key)
    resp = requests.get(url)
    results = resp.json()
    count  = 0
    for p in results['photos']['photo']:
        if count >= max_count:
            return photo_collection
        print 'Processing photo: "%s"' % p['title']
        photo = {}
        url = "http://api.flickr.com/services/rest/?method=flickr.
photos.getInfo&photo_id=" + p['id'] + "&format=json&nojsoncallback=1&a
pi_key=" + api_key
        info = requests.get(url).json()
        photo["flickrid"] = p['id']
        photo["title"] = info['photo']['title']['_content']
        photo["description"] = info['photo']['description']['_
content']
        photo["page_url"] = info['photo']['urls']['url'][0]['_
content']

        photo["farm"] = info['photo']['farm']
        photo["server"] = info['photo']['server']
        photo["secret"] = info['photo']['secret']

        # comments
        numcomments = int(info['photo']['comments']['_content'])
        if numcomments:
            #print "   Now reading comments (%d)..." % numcomments
            url = "http://api.flickr.com/services/rest/?method=flickr.
photos.comments.getList&photo_id=" + p['id'] + "&format=json&nojsoncal
lback=1&api_key=" + api_key
            comments = requests.get(url).json()
```

```
            photo["comment"] = []
            for c in comments['comments']['comment']:
                comment = {}
                comment["body"] = c['_content']
                comment["authorid"] = c['author']
                comment["authorname"] = c['authorname']
                photo["comment"].append(comment)
        photo_collection.append(photo)
        count = count + 1
    return photo_collection


if __name__ == '__main__':
    parser = argparse.ArgumentParser(description='Get photo info from 
Flickr')
    parser.add_argument('--api-key', action="store", dest="api_key", 
default=flickr_apikey)
    parser.add_argument('--tag', action="store", dest="tag", 
default='Python')
    parser.add_argument('--max-count', action="store", dest="max_
count", default=3, type=int)
    # parse arguments
    given_args = parser.parse_args()
    api_key, tag, max_count =  given_args.api_key, given_args.tag, 
given_args.max_count
    photo_info = collect_photo_info(api_key, tag, max_count)
    for photo in photo_info:
        for k,v in photo.iteritems():
            if k == "title":
                print "Showing photo info...."
            elif k == "comment":
                "\tPhoto got %s comments." %len(v)
            else:
                print "\t%s => %s" %(k,v)
```

You can run this recipe with your Flickr API key either by placing it in a `local_settings.py` file or supplying it from the command line (via the `--api-key` argument). In addition to the API key, a search tag and maximum count of the result arguments can be supplied. By default, this recipe will search for the `Python` tag and restrict the result to three entries, as shown in the following output:

```
$ python 8_4_get_flickr_photo_info.py
Processing photo: "legolas"
Processing photo: ""The Dance of the Hunger of Kaa""
Processing photo: "Rocky"
    description => Stimson Python
```

```
Showiing photo info....
    farm => 8
    server => 7402
    secret => 6cbae671b5
    flickrid => 10054626824
    page_url => http://www.flickr.com/photos/102763809@N03/10054626824/
    description => &quot; 'Good. Begins now the dance--the Dance of the
Hunger of Kaa. Sit still and watch.'


He turned twice or thrice in a big circle, weaving his head from right to
left.
Then he began making loops and figures of eight with his body, and soft,
oozy triangles that melted into squares and five-sided figures, and
coiled mounds, never resting, never hurrying, and never stopping his
low humming song. It grew darker and darker, till at last the dragging,
shifting coils disappeared, but they could hear the rustle of the
scales.&quot;
(From &quot;Kaa's Hunting&quot; in &quot;The Jungle Book&quot; (1893) by
Rudyard Kipling)


These old abandoned temples built around the 12th century belong to the
abandoned city which inspired Kipling's Jungle Book.
They are rising at the top of a mountain which dominates the jungle at
811 meters above sea level in the centre of the jungle of Bandhavgarh
located in the Indian state Madhya Pradesh.
Baghel King Vikramaditya Singh abandoned Bandhavgarh fort in 1617 when
Rewa, at a distance of 130 km was established as a capital.
Abandonment allowed wildlife development in this region.
When Baghel Kings became aware of it, he declared Bandhavgarh as their
hunting preserve and strictly prohibited tree cutting and wildlife
hunting...


Join the photographer at <a href="http://www.facebook.com/laurent.
goldstein.photography" rel="nofollow">www.facebook.com/laurent.goldstein.
photography</a>


© All photographs are copyrighted and all rights reserved.
Please do not use any photographs without permission (even for private
use).
The use of any work without consent of the artist is PROHIBITED and will
lead automatically to consequences.
```

```
Showiing photo info....
    farm => 6
    server => 5462
    secret => 6f9c0e7f83
    flickrid => 10051136944
    page_url => http://www.flickr.com/photos/designldg/10051136944/
    description => Ball Python
Showiing photo info....
    farm => 4
    server => 3744
    secret => 529840767f
    flickrid => 10046353675
    page_url =>
http://www.flickr.com/photos/megzzdollphotos/10046353675/
```

How it works...

This recipe demonstrates how to interact with Flickr using its REST APIs. In this example, the `collect_photo_info()` tag takes three parameters: Flickr API key, a search tag, and the desired number of search results.

We construct the first URL to search for photos. Note that in this URL, the value of the method parameter is `flickr.photos.search` and the desired result format is JSON.

The results of the first `get()` call are stored in the `resp` variable and then converted to the JSON format by calling the `json()` method on `resp`. Now, the JSON data is read in a loop looking into the `['photos']['photo']` iterator. A `photo_collection` list is created to return the result after organizing the information. In this list, each photo information is represented by a dictionary. The keys of this dictionary are populated by extracting information from the earlier JSON response and another `GET` request to get the information regarding the specific photo.

Note that to get the comments about a photo, we need to make another `get()` request and gather comment information from the `['comments']['comment']` elements of the returned JSON. Finally, these comments are appended to a list and attached to the photo dictionary entry.

In the main function, we extract the `photo_collection` dictionary and print some useful information about each photo.

Searching for SOAP methods from an Amazon S3 web service

If you need to interact with a server that implements web services in Simple Object Access Procedure (SOAP), then this recipe can help to get a starting point.

Getting ready

We can use the third-party `SOAPpy` library for this task. This can be installed by running the following command:

```
$pip install SOAPpy
```

How to do it...

We create a proxy instance and introspect the server methods before we can call them.

In this recipe, let's interact with an Amazon S3 storage service. We have got a test URL for the web services API. An API key is necessary to do this simple task.

Listing 8.5 gives the code for searching for SOAP methods from an Amazon S3 web service, as shown:

```
#!/usr/bin/env python
# Python Network Programming Cookbook -- Chapter - 8
# This program is optimized for Python 2.7.
# It may run on any other version with/without modifications.

import SOAPpy

TEST_URL = 'http://s3.amazonaws.com/ec2-downloads/2009-04-04.ec2.wsdl'

def list_soap_methods(url):
    proxy = SOAPpy.WSDL.Proxy(url)
    print '%d methods in WSDL:' % len(proxy.methods) + '\n'
    for key in proxy.methods.keys():
  "Key Details:"
        for k,v in proxy.methods[key].__dict__.iteritems():
            print "%s ==> %s" %(k,v)


if __name__ == '__main__':
    list_soap_methods(TEST_URL)
```

If you run this script, it will print the total number of available methods that support web services definition language (WSDL) and the details of one arbitrary method, as shown:

```
$ python 8_5_search_amazonaws_with_SOAP.py
/home/faruq/env/lib/python2.7/site-packages/wstools/XMLSchema.py:1280:
UserWarning: annotation is
ignored
  warnings.warn('annotation is ignored')
43 methods in WSDL:

Key Name: ReleaseAddress
Key Details:
    encodingStyle ==> None
    style ==> document
    methodName ==> ReleaseAddress
    retval ==> None
    soapAction ==> ReleaseAddress
    namespace ==> None
    use ==> literal
    location ==> https://ec2.amazonaws.com/
    inparams ==> [<wstools.WSDLTools.ParameterInfo instance at
0x8fb9d0c>]
    outheaders ==> []
    inheaders ==> []
    transport ==> http://schemas.xmlsoap.org/soap/http
    outparams ==> [<wstools.WSDLTools.ParameterInfo instance at
0x8fb9d2c>]
```

How it works...

This script defines a method called `list_soap_methods()` that takes a URL and constructs a SOAP proxy object by calling the `WSDL.Proxy()` method of `SOAPpy`. The available SOAP methods are available under this proxy's method attribute.

An iteration over the proxy's method keys are done to introspect the method keys. A `for` loop just prints the details of a single SOAP method, that is, the name of the key and details about it.

Searching Google for custom information

Searching Google for getting information about something seems to be an everyday activity for many people. Let's try to search Google for some information.

Getting ready

This recipe uses a third-party Python library, `requests`, which can be installed via `pip`, as shown in the following command:

```
$ pip install SOAPpy
```

How to do it...

Google has sophisticated APIs to conduct a search. However, they require you to register and get the API keys by following a specific way. For simplicity's sake, let us use Google's old plain **Asynchronous JavaScript** (**AJAX**) API to search for some information about Python books.

Listing 8.6 gives the code for searching Google for custom information, as shown:

```
#!/usr/bin/env python
# Python Network Programming Cookbook -- Chapter - 8
# This program is optimized for Python 2.7.# It may run on any other
version with/without modifications.
import argparse
import json
import urllib
import requests

BASE_URL = 'http://ajax.googleapis.com/ajax/services/search/web?v=1.0'

def get_search_url(query):
  return "%s&%s" %(BASE_URL, query)

def search_info(tag):
  query = urllib.urlencode({'q': tag})
  url = get_search_url(query)
  response = requests.get(url)
  results = response.json()

  data = results['responseData']
  print 'Found total results: %s' %
data['cursor']['estimatedResultCount']
  hits = data['results']
  print 'Found top %d hits:' % len(hits)
  for h in hits:
```

```
        print ' ', h['url']
        print 'More results available from %s' %
    data['cursor']['moreResultsUrl']


    if __name__ == '__main__':
      parser = argparse.ArgumentParser(description='Search info from
    Google')
      parser.add_argument('--tag', action="store", dest="tag",
    default='Python books')
      # parse arguments
      given_args = parser.parse_args()
      search_info(given_args.tag)
```

If you run this script by specifying a search query in the `--tag` argument, then it will search Google and print a total results count and the top four hits pages, as shown:

```
$ python 8_6_search_products_from_Google.py
Found total results: 12300000
Found top 4 hits:
  https://wiki.python.org/moin/PythonBooks
  http://www.amazon.com/Python-Languages-Tools-Programming-
Books/b%3Fie%3DUTF8%26node%3D285856
  http://pythonbooks.revolunet.com/
  http://readwrite.com/2011/03/25/python-is-an-increasingly-popu
More results available from
http://www.google.com/search?oe=utf8&ie=utf8&source=uds&start=0&hl=en
&q=Python+books
```

How it works...

In this recipe, we defined a short function, `get_search_url()`, which constructs the search URL from a `BASE_URL` constant and the target query.

The main search function, `search_info()`, takes the search tag and constructs the query. The `requests` library is used to make the `get()` call. The returned response is then turned into JSON data.

The search results are extracted from the JSON data by accessing the value of the `'responseData'` key. The estimated results and hits are then extracted by accessing the relevant keys of the result data. The first four hit URLs are then printed on the screen.

Searching Amazon for books through product search API

If you like to search for products on Amazon and include some of them in your website or application, this recipe can help you to do that. We can see how to search Amazon for books.

Getting ready

This recipe depends on the third-party Python library, `bottlenose`. You can install this library using `pip`, as shown in the following command:

```
$ pip install  bottlenose
```

First, you need to place your Amazon account's access key, secret key, and affiliate ID into `local_settings.py`. A sample settings file is provided with the book code. You can also edit this script and place it here as well.

How to do it...

We can use the `bottlenose` library that implements the Amazon's product search APIs.

Listing 8.7 gives the code for searching Amazon for books through product search APIs, as shown:

```
#!/usr/bin/env python
# Python Network Programming Cookbook -- Chapter - 8
# This program is optimized for Python 2.7.
# It may run on any other version with/without modifications.

import argparse
import bottlenose
from xml.dom import minidom as xml

try:
  from local_settings import amazon_account
except ImportError:
  pass

ACCESS_KEY = amazon_account['access_key']
SECRET_KEY = amazon_account['secret_key']
AFFILIATE_ID = amazon_account['affiliate_id']
```

```
def search_for_books(tag, index):
  """Search Amazon for Books """
  amazon = bottlenose.Amazon(ACCESS_KEY, SECRET_KEY, AFFILIATE_ID)
  results = amazon.ItemSearch(
    SearchIndex = index,
    Sort = "relevancerank",
    Keywords = tag
  )
  parsed_result = xml.parseString(results)

  all_items = []
  attrs = ['Title','Author', 'URL']

  for item in parsed_result.getElementsByTagName('Item'):
    parse_item = {}

  for attr in attrs:
    parse_item[attr] = ""
    try:
      parse_item[attr] =
item.getElementsByTagName(attr)[0].childNodes[0].data
    except:
      pass
    all_items.append(parse_item)
  return all_items

if __name__ == '__main__':
  parser = argparse.ArgumentParser(description='Search info from
Amazon')
  parser.add_argument('--tag', action="store", dest="tag",
default='Python')
  parser.add_argument('--index', action="store", dest="index",
default='Books')
  # parse arguments
  given_args = parser.parse_args()
  books = search_for_books(given_args.tag, given_args.index)

  for book in books:
    for k,v in book.iteritems():
      print "%s: %s" %(k,v)
      print "-" * 80
```

If you run this recipe with a search tag and index, you can see some results similar to the following output:

```
$ python 8_7_search_amazon_for_books.py --tag=Python --index=Books
URL: http://www.amazon.com/Python-In-Day-Basics-Coding/dp/tech-data/1
490475575%3FSubscriptionId%3DAKIAIPPW3IK76PBRLWBA%26tag%3D7052-6929-
7878%26linkCode%3Dxm2%26camp%3D2025%26creative%3D386001%26creative-
ASIN%3D1490475575
Author: Richard Wagstaff
Title: Python In A Day: Learn The Basics, Learn It Quick, Start Coding
Fast (In A Day Books) (Volume 1)
-----------------------------------------------------------------
-------
URL: http://www.amazon.com/Learning-Python-Mark-Lutz/dp/tech-data/1449355
730%3FSubscriptionId%3DAKIAIPPW3IK76PBRLWBA%26tag%3D7052-6929-7878%26link
Code%3Dxm2%26camp%3D2025%26creative%3D386001%26creativeASIN%3D1449355730
Author: Mark Lutz
Title: Learning Python
-----------------------------------------------------------------
-------
URL: http://www.amazon.com/Python-Programming-Introduction-Computer-
Science/dp/tech-data/1590282418%3FSubscriptionId%3DAKIAIPPW3IK76PBRLWBA%2
6tag%3D7052-6929-7878%26linkCode%3Dxm2%26camp%3D2025%26creative%3D386001%
26creativeASIN%3D1590282418
Author: John Zelle
Title: Python Programming: An Introduction to Computer Science 2nd
Edition
-------------------------------------------------------------
-----------
```

How it works...

This recipe uses the third-party `bottlenose` library's `Amazon()` class to create an object for searching Amazon through the product search API. This is done by the top-level `search_for_books()` function. The `ItemSearch()` method of this object is invoked with passing values to the `SearchIndex` and `Keywords` keys. It uses the `relevancerank` method to sort the search results.

The search results are processed using the `xml` module's `minidom` interface, which has a useful `parseString()` method. It returns the parsed XML tree-like data structure. The `getElementsByTagName()` method on this data structure helps to find the item's information. The item attributes are then looked up and placed in a dictionary of parsed items. Finally, all the parsed items are appended in a `all_items()` list and returned to the user.

9
Network Monitoring and Security

In this chapter, we will cover the following recipes:

- Sniffing packets on your network
- Saving packets in the pcap format using the pcap dumper
- Adding an extra header in HTTP packets
- Scanning the ports of a remote host
- Customizing the IP address of a packet
- Replaying traffic by reading from a saved pcap file
- Scanning the broadcast of packets

Introduction

This chapter presents some interesting Python recipes for network security monitoring and vulnerability scanning. We begin by sniffing packets on a network using the `pcap` library. Then, we start using `Scapy`, which is a Swiss knife type of library that can do many similar tasks. Some common tasks in packet analysis are presented using `Scapy`, such as saving a packet in the `pcap` format, adding an extra header, and modifying the IP address of a packet.

Some other advanced tasks on network intrusion detection are also included in this chapter, for example, replaying traffic from a saved `pcap` file and broadcast scanning.

Sniffing packets on your network

If you are interested in sniffing packets on your local network, this recipe can be used as the starting point. Remember that you may not be able to sniff packets other than what is destined to your machine, as decent network switches will only forward traffic that is designated to your machine.

Getting ready

You need to install the `pylibpcap` library (Version 0.6.4 or greater) for this recipe to work. It's available at SourceForge (`http://sourceforge.net/projects/pylibpcap/`).

You also need to install the `construct` library, which can be installed from PyPI via `pip` or `easy_install`, as shown in the following command:

```
$ easy_install construct
```

How to do it...

We can supply command-line arguments, for example, the network interface name and TCP port number, for sniffing.

Listing 9.1 gives the code for sniffing packets on your network, as follows:

```
#!/usr/bin/env python
# Python Network Programming Cookbook -- Chapter - 9
# This program is optimized for Python 2.6.
# It may run on any other version with/without modifications.

import argparse
import pcap
from construct.protocols.ipstack import ip_stack


def print_packet(pktlen, data, timestamp):
  """ Callback for printing the packet payload"""
  if not data:
    return

  stack = ip_stack.parse(data)
  payload = stack.next.next.next
  print payload
```

```
def main():
  # setup commandline arguments
  parser = argparse.ArgumentParser(description='Packet Sniffer')
  parser.add_argument('--iface', action="store", dest="iface",
default='eth0')
  parser.add_argument('--port', action="store", dest="port",
default=80, type=int)
  # parse arguments
  given_args = parser.parse_args()
  iface, port =  given_args.iface, given_args.port
  # start sniffing
  pc = pcap.pcapObject()
  pc.open_live(iface, 1600, 0, 100)
  pc.setfilter('dst port %d' %port, 0, 0)

  print 'Press CTRL+C to end capture'
  try:
    while True:
      pc.dispatch(1, print_packet)
  except KeyboardInterrupt:
    print 'Packet statistics: %d packets received, %d packets
dropped, %d packets dropped by the interface' % pc.stats()

if __name__ == '__main__':
  main()
```

If you run this script passing the command-line arguments, `--iface=eth0` and `--port=80`, this script will sniff all the HTTP packets from your web browser. So, after running this script, if you access `http://www.google.com` on your browser, you can then see a raw packet output like the following:

```
python 9_1_packet_sniffer.py --iface=eth0 --port=80
Press CTRL+C to end capture
''
0000   47 45 54 20 2f 20 48 54 54 50 2f 31 2e 31 0d 0a   GET / HTTP/1.1..
0010   48 6f 73 74 3a 20 77 77 77 2e 67 6f 6f 67 6c 65   Host: www.google
0020   2e 63 6f 6d 0d 0a 43 6f 6e 6e 65 63 74 69 6f 6e   .com..Connection
0030   3a 20 6b 65 65 70 2d 61 6c 69 76 65 0d 0a 41 63   : keep-alive..Ac
0040   63 65 70 74 3a 20 74 65 78 74 2f 68 74 6d 6c 2c   cept: text/html,
0050   61 70 70 6c 69 63 61 74 69 6f 6e 2f 78 68 74 6d   application/xhtm
0060   6c 2b 78 6d 6c 2c 61 70 70 6c 69 63 61 74 69 6f   l+xml,applicatio
0070   6e 2f 78 6d 6c 3b 71 3d 30 2e 39 2c 2a 2f 2a 3b   n/xml;q=0.9,*/*;
0080   71 3d 30 2e 38 0d 0a 55 73 65 72 2d 41 67 65 6e   q=0.8..User-Agen
```

```
0090    74 3a 20 4d 6f 7a 69 6c 6c 61 2f 35 2e 30 20 28    t: Mozilla/5.0 (
00A0    58 31 31 3b 20 4c 69 6e 75 78 20 69 36 38 36 29    X11; Linux i686)
00B0    20 41 70 70 6c 65 57 65 62 4b 69 74 2f 35 33 37     AppleWebKit/537
00C0    2e 33 31 20 28 4b 48 54 4d 4c 2c 20 6c 69 6b 65    .31 (KHTML, like
00D0    20 47 65 63 6b 6f 29 20 43 68 72 6f 6d 65 2f 32     Gecko) Chrome/2
00E0    36 2e 30 2e 31 34 31 30 2e 34 33 20 53 61 66 61    6.0.1410.43 Safa
00F0    72 69 2f 35 33 37 2e 33 31 0d 0a 58 2d 43 68 72    ri/537.31..X-Chr
0100    6f 6d 65 2d 56 61 72 69 61 74 69 6f 6e 73 3a 20    ome-Variations:
0110    43 50 71 31 79 51 45 49 6b 62 62 4a 41 51 69 59    CPq1yQEIkbbJAQiY
0120    74 73 6b 42 43 4b 4f 32 79 51 45 49 70 37 62 4a    tskBCKO2yQEIp7bJ
0130    41 51 69 70 74 73 6b 42 43 4c 65 32 79 51 45 49    AQiptskBCLe2yQEI
0140    2b 6f 50 4b 41 51 3d 3d 0d 0a 44 4e 54 3a 20 31    +oPKAQ==..DNT: 1
0150    0d 0a 41 63 63 65 70 74 2d 45 6e 63 6f 64 69 6e    ..Accept-Encodin
0160    67 3a 20 67 7a 69 70 2c 64 65 66 6c 61 74 65 2c    g: gzip,deflate,
0170    73 64 63 68 0d 0a 41 63 63 65 70 74 2d 4c 61 6e    sdch..Accept-Lan
0180    67 75 61 67 65 3a 20 65 6e 2d 47 42 2c 65 6e 2d    guage: en-GB,en-
0190    55 53 3b 71 3d 30 2e 38 2c 65 6e 3b 71 3d 30 2e    US;q=0.8,en;q=0.
01A0    36 0d 0a 41 63 63 65 70 74 2d 43 68 61 72 73 65    6..Accept-Charse
01B0    74 3a 20 49 53 4f 2d 38 38 35 39 2d 31 2c 75 74    t: ISO-8859-1,ut
01C0    66 2d 38 3b 71 3d 30 2e 37 2c 2a 3b 71 3d 30 2e    f-8;q=0.7,*;q=0.
01D0    33 0d 0a 43 6f 6f 6b 69 65 3a 20 50 52 45 46 3d    3..Cookie: PREF=

....

^CPacket statistics: 17 packets received, 0 packets dropped, 0
packets dropped by the interface
```

How it works...

This recipe relies on the `pcapObject()` class from the `pcap` library to create an instance of sniffer. In the `main()` method, an instance of this class is created, and a filter is set using the `setfilter()` method so that only the HTTP packets are captured. Finally, the `dispatch()` method starts sniffing and sends the sniffed packet to the `print_packet()` function for postprocessing.

In the `print_packet()` function, if a packet has data, the payload is extracted using the `ip_stack.parse()` method from the `construct` library. This library is useful for low-level data processing.

Saving packets in the pcap format using the pcap dumper

The **pcap** format, abbreviated from **packet capture**, is a common file format for saving network data. More details on the pcap format can be found at `http://wiki.wireshark.org/Development/LibpcapFileFormat`.

If you want to save your captured network packets to a file and later re-use them for further processing, this recipe can be a working example for you.

How to do it...

In this recipe, we use the `Scapy` library to sniff packets and write to a file. All utility functions and definitions of `Scapy` can be imported using the wild card import, as shown in the following command:

```
from scapy.all import *
```

This is only for demonstration purposes and not recommended for production code.

The `sniff()` function of `Scapy` takes the name of a callback function. Let's write a callback function that will write the packets onto a file.

Listing 9.2 gives the code for saving packets in the pcap format using the pcap dumper, as follows:

```
#!/usr/bin/env python
# Python Network Programming Cookbook -- Chapter - 9
# This program is optimized for Python 2.7.
# It may run on any other version with/without modifications.

import os
from scapy.all import *

pkts = []
iter = 0
pcapnum = 0

def write_cap(x):
  global pkts
  global iter
  global pcapnum
  pkts.append(x)
  iter += 1
  if iter == 3:
```

```
        pcapnum += 1
        pname = "pcap%d.pcap" % pcapnum
        wrpcap(pname, pkts)
        pkts = []
        iter = 0

if __name__ == '__main__':
  print "Started packet capturing and dumping... Press CTRL+C to exit"
  sniff(prn=write_cap)

  print "Testing the dump file..."
  dump_file = "./pcap1.pcap"
  if os.path.exists(dump_file):
    print "dump fie %s found." %dump_file
    pkts = sniff(offline=dump_file)
    count = 0
    while (count <=2):
      print "----Dumping pkt:%s----" %count
      print hexdump(pkts[count])
      count += 1
  else:
    print "dump fie %s not found." %dump_file
```

If you run this script, you will see an output similar to the following:

```
# python 9_2_save_packets_in_pcap_format.py
^CStarted packet capturing and dumping... Press CTRL+C to exit
Testing the dump file...
dump fie ./pcap1.pcap found.
----Dumping pkt:0----
0000   08 00 27 95 0D 1A 52 54  00 12 35 02 08 00 45 00   ..'...
RT..5...E.
0010   00 DB E2 6D 00 00 40 06  7C 9E 6C A0 A2 62 0A 00
...m..@.|.l..b..
0020   02 0F 00 50 99 55 97 98  2C 84 CE 45 9B 6C 50 18
...P.U..,..E.lP.
0030   FF FF 53 E0 00 00 48 54  54 50 2F 31 2E 31 20 32   ..S...HTTP/1.1
2
0040   30 30 20 4F 4B 0D 0A 58  2D 44 42 2D 54 69 6D 65   00 OK..X-DB-
Time
0050   6F 75 74 3A 20 31 32 30  0D 0A 50 72 61 67 6D 61   out: 120..
Pragma
0060   3A 20 6E 6F 2D 63 61 63  68 65 0D 0A 43 61 63 68   : no-cache..
Cach
```

```
0070   65 2D 43 6F 6E 74 72 6F  6C 3A 20 6E 6F 2D 63 61   e-Control: no-
ca
0080   63 68 65 0D 0A 43 6F 6E  74 65 6E 74 2D 54 79 70   che..Content-
Typ
0090   65 3A 20 74 65 78 74 2F  70 6C 61 69 6E 0D 0A 44   e: text/
plain..D
00a0   61 74 65 3A 20 53 75 6E  2C 20 31 35 20 53 65 70   ate: Sun, 15
Sep
00b0   20 32 30 31 33 20 31 35  3A 32 32 3A 33 36 20 47    2013 15:22:36
G
00c0   4D 54 0D 0A 43 6F 6E 74  65 6E 74 2D 4C 65 6E 67   MT..Content-
Leng
00d0   74 68 3A 20 31 35 0D 0A  0D 0A 7B 22 72 65 74 22   th: 15....
{"ret"
00e0   3A 20 22 70 75 6E 74 22  7D                        : "punt"}
None
----Dumping pkt:1----
0000   52 54 00 12 35 02 08 00  27 95 0D 1A 08 00 45 00
RT..5...'.....E.
0010   01 D2 1F 25 40 00 40 06  FE EF 0A 00 02 0F 6C A0
...%@.@.......l.
0020   A2 62 99 55 00 50 CE 45  9B 6C 97 98 2D 37 50 18   .b.U.P.E.l..-
7P.
0030   F9 28 1C D6 00 00 47 45  54 20 2F 73 75 62 73 63   .(....GET /
subsc
0040   72 69 62 65 3F 68 6F 73  74 5F 69 6E 74 3D 35 31   ribe?host_
int=51
0050   30 35 36 34 37 34 36 26  6E 73 5F 6D 61 70 3D 31   0564746&ns_
map=1
0060   36 30 36 39 36 39 39 34  5F 33 30 30 38 30 38 34
60696994_3008084
0070   30 37 37 31 34 2C 31 30  31 39 34 36 31 31 5F 31
07714,10194611_1
0080   31 30 35 33 30 39 38 34  33 38 32 30 32 31 31 2C
105309843820211,
0090   31 34 36 34 32 38 30 35  32 5F 33 32 39 34 33 38
146428052_329438
00a0   36 33 34 34 30 38 34 2C  31 31 36 30 31 35 33 31
6344084,11601531
00b0   5F 32 37 39 31 38 34 34  37 35 37 37 31 2C 31 30
_279184475771,10
00c0   31 39 34 38 32 38 5F 33  30 30 37 34 39 36 35 39
194828_300749659
00d0   30 30 2C 33 33 30 39 39  31 39 38 32 5F 38 31 39
```

```
00,330991982_819
00e0    33 35 33 37 30 36 30 36  2C 31 36 33 32 37 38 35
35370606,1632785
00f0    35 5F 31 32 39 30 31 32  32 39 37 34 33 26 75 73
5_12901229743&us
0100    65 72 5F 69 64 3D 36 35  32 30 33 37 32 26 6E 69   er_
id=6520372&ni
0110    64 3D 32 26 74 73 3D 31  33 37 39 32 35 38 35 36
d=2&ts=137925856
0120    31 20 48 54 54 50 2F 31  2E 31 0D 0A 48 6F 73 74   1 HTTP/1.1..
Host
0130    3A 20 6E 6F 74 69 66 79  33 2E 64 72 6F 70 62 6F   : notify3.
dropbo
0140    78 2E 63 6F 6D 0D 0A 41  63 63 65 70 74 2D 45 6E   x.com..Accept-
En
0150    63 6F 64 69 6E 67 3A 20  69 64 65 6E 74 69 74 79   coding:
identity
0160    0D 0A 43 6F 6E 6E 65 63  74 69 6F 6E 3A 20 6B 65   ..Connection:
ke
0170    65 70 2D 61 6C 69 76 65  0D 0A 58 2D 44 72 6F 70   ep-alive..X-
Drop
0180    62 6F 78 2D 4C 6F 63 61  6C 65 3A 20 65 6E 5F 55   box-Locale:
en_U
0190    53 0D 0A 55 73 65 72 2D  41 67 65 6E 74 3A 20 44   S..User-Agent:
D
01a0    72 6F 70 62 6F 78 44 65  73 6B 74 6F 70 43 6C 69
ropboxDesktopCli
01b0    65 6E 74 2F 32 2E 30 2E  32 32 20 28 4C 69 6E 75   ent/2.0.22
(Linu
01c0    78 3B 20 32 2E 36 2E 33  32 2D 35 2D 36 38 36 3B   x; 2.6.32-5-
686;
01d0    20 69 33 32 3B 20 65 6E  5F 55 53 29 0D 0A 0D 0A    i32; en_
US)....
None
----Dumping pkt:2----
0000    08 00 27 95 0D 1A 52 54  00 12 35 02 08 00 45 00   ..'...
RT..5...E.
0010    00 28 E2 6E 00 00 40 06  7D 50 6C A0 A2 62 0A 00   .(.n..@.}
Pl..b..
0020    02 0F 00 50 99 55 97 98  2D 37 CE 45 9D 16 50 10   ...P.U..-
7.E..P.
0030    FF FF CA F1 00 00 00 00  00 00 00 00               ............
None
```

How it works...

This recipe uses the `sniff()` and `wrpacp()` utility functions of the `Scapy` library to capture all the network packets and dump them onto a file. After capturing a packet via `sniff()`, the `write_cap()` function is called on that packet. Some global variables are used to work on packets one after another. For example, packets are stored in a `pkts[]` list and packet and variable counts are used. When the value of the count is 3, the `pkts` list is dumped onto a file named `pcap1.pcap`, the count variable is reset so that we can continue capturing another three packets and dumped onto `pcap2.pcap`, and so on.

In the `test_dump_file()` function, assume the presence of the first dump file, `pcap1.dump`, in the working directory. Now, `sniff()` is used with an offline parameter, which captured packets from the file instead of network. Here, the packets are decoded one after another using the `hexdump()` function. The contents of the packets are then printed on the screen.

Adding an extra header in HTTP packets

Sometimes, you would like to manipulate an application by supplying a custom HTTP header that contains custom information. For example, adding an authorization header can be useful to implement the HTTP basic authentication in your packet capture code.

How to do it...

Let us sniff the packets using the `sniff()` function of `Scapy` and define a callback function, `modify_packet_header()`, which adds an extra header of certain packets.

Listing 9.3 gives the code for adding an extra header in HTTP packets, as follows:

```
#!/usr/bin/env python
# Python Network Programming Cookbook -- Chapter - 9
# This program is optimized for Python 2.7.
# It may run on any other version with/without modifications.

from scapy.all import *

def modify_packet_header(pkt):
  """ Parse the header and add an extra header"""
  if pkt.haslayer(TCP) and pkt.getlayer(TCP).dport == 80 and
pkt.haslayer(Raw):
    hdr = pkt[TCP].payload.__dict__
    extra_item = {'Extra Header' : ' extra value'}
    hdr.update(extra_item)
    send_hdr = '\r\n'.join(hdr)
    pkt[TCP].payload = send_hdr
```

```
        pkt.show()

        del pkt[IP].chksum
        send(pkt)

if __name__ == '__main__':
    # start sniffing
    sniff(filter="tcp and ( port 80 )", prn=modify_packet_header)
```

If you run this script, it will show a captured packet; print the modified version of it and send it to the network, as shown in the following output. This can be verified by other packet capturing tools such as `tcpdump` or `wireshark`:

```
$ python 9_3_add_extra_http_header_in_sniffed_packet.py

###[ Ethernet ]###
  dst       = 52:54:00:12:35:02
  src       = 08:00:27:95:0d:1a
  type      = 0x800
###[ IP ]###
     version   = 4L
     ihl       = 5L
     tos       = 0x0
     len       = 525
     id        = 13419
     flags     = DF
     frag      = 0L
     ttl       = 64
     proto     = tcp
     chksum    = 0x171
     src       = 10.0.2.15
     dst       = 82.94.164.162
     \options   \
###[ TCP ]###
        sport     = 49273
        dport     = www
        seq       = 107715690
        ack       = 216121024
        dataofs   = 5L
        reserved  = 0L
        flags     = PA
        window    = 6432
```

```
        chksum    = 0x50f
        urgptr    = 0
        options   = []
###[ Raw ]###
           load      = 'Extra Header\r\nsent_time\r\nfields\r\
naliastypes\r\npost_transforms\r\nunderlayer\r\nfieldtype\r\ntime\r\
ninitialized\r\noverloaded_fields\r\npacketfields\r\npayload\r\ndefault_
fields'
.
Sent 1 packets.
```

How it works...

First, we set up the packet sniffing using the `sniff()` function of **Scapy**, specifying `modify_packet_header()` as the callback function for each packet. All TCP packets having TCP and a raw layer that are destined to port `80` (HTTP) are considered for modification. So, the current packet header is extracted from the packet's payload data.

The extra header is then appended to the existing header dictionary. The packet is then printed on screen using the `show()` method, and for avoiding the correctness checking failure, the packet checksum data is removed from the packet. Finally, the packet is sent over the network.

Scanning the ports of a remote host

If you are trying to connect to a remote host using a particular port, sometimes you get the message saying that `Connection is refused`. The reason for this is that, most likely, the server is down on the remote host. In such a situation, you can try to see whether the port is open or in the listening state. You can scan multiple ports to identify the available services in a machine.

How to do it...

Using Python's standard socket library, we can accomplish this port-scanning task. We can take three command-line arguments: target host, and start and end port numbers.

Listing 9.4 gives the code for scanning the ports of a remote host, as follows:

```
#!/usr/bin/env python
# Python Network Programming Cookbook -- Chapter - 9
# This program is optimized for Python 2.7.
# It may run on any other version with/without modifications.
```

```
import argparse
import socket
import sys

def scan_ports(host, start_port, end_port):
  """ Scan remote hosts """
  #Create socket
  try:
    sock = socket.socket(socket.AF_INET,socket.SOCK_STREAM)
  except socket.error,err_msg:
    print 'Socket creation failed. Error code: '+ str(err_msg[0])
+ ' Error mesage: ' + err_msg[1]
    sys.exit()

  #Get IP of remote host
  try:
    remote_ip = socket.gethostbyname(host)
  except socket.error,error_msg:
    print error_msg
  sys.exit()

  #Scan ports
  end_port += 1
  for port in range(start_port,end_port):
    try:
      sock.connect((remote_ip,port))
      print 'Port ' + str(port) + ' is open'
      sock.close()
      sock = socket.socket(socket.AF_INET,socket.SOCK_STREAM)
    except socket.error:
      pass # skip various socket errors

if __name__ == '__main__':
  # setup commandline arguments
  parser = argparse.ArgumentParser(description='Remote Port
Scanner')
  parser.add_argument('--host', action="store", dest="host",
default='localhost')
  parser.add_argument('--start-port', action="store",
dest="start_port", default=1, type=int)
  parser.add_argument('--end-port', action="store",
dest="end_port", default=100, type=int)
  # parse arguments
  given_args = parser.parse_args()
  host, start_port, end_port =  given_args.host,
given_args.start_port, given_args.end_port
  scan_ports(host, start_port, end_port)
```

If you run this recipe to scan your local machine's port 1 to 100 to detect open ports, you will get an output similar to the following:

```
# python 9_4_scan_port_of_a_remote_host.py --host=localhost --start-port=1 --end-port=100
Port 21 is open
Port 22 is open
Port 23 is open
Port 25 is open
Port 80 is open
```

How it works...

This recipe demonstrates how to scan open ports of a machine using Python's standard socket library. The `scan_port()` function takes three arguments: hostname, start port, and end port. Then, it scans the entire port range in three steps.

Create a TCP socket using the `socket()` function.

If the socket is created successfully, then resolve the IP address of the remote host using the `gethostbyname()` function.

If the target host's IP address is found, try to connect to the IP using the `connect()` function. If that's successful, then it implies that the port is open. Now, close the port with the `close()` function and repeat the first step for the next port.

Customizing the IP address of a packet

If you ever need to create a network packet and customize the source and destination IP or ports, this recipe can serve as the starting point.

How to do it...

We can take all the useful command-line arguments such as network interface name, protocol name, source IP, source port, destination IP, destination port, and optional TCP flags.

We can use the `Scapy` library to create a custom TCP or UDP packet and send it over the network.

Listing 9.5 gives the code for customizing the IP address of a packet, as follows:

```
#!/usr/bin/env python
# Python Network Programming Cookbook -- Chapter - 9
# This program is optimized for Python 2.7.
# It may run on any other version with/without modifications.
```

```
import argparse
import sys
import re
from random import randint

from scapy.all import IP,TCP,UDP,conf,send


def send_packet(protocol=None, src_ip=None, src_port=None, flags=None,
dst_ip=None, dst_port=None, iface=None):
  """Modify and send an IP packet."""
  if protocol == 'tcp':
    packet = IP(src=src_ip, dst=dst_ip)/TCP(flags=flags,
sport=src_port, dport=dst_port)
  elif protocol == 'udp':
  if flags: raise Exception(" Flags are not supported for udp")
    packet = IP(src=src_ip, dst=dst_ip)/UDP(sport=src_port,
dport=dst_port)
  else:
    raise Exception("Unknown protocol %s" % protocol)

  send(packet, iface=iface)


if __name__ == '__main__':
  # setup commandline arguments
  parser = argparse.ArgumentParser(description='Packet Modifier')
  parser.add_argument('--iface', action="store", dest="iface",
default='eth0')
  parser.add_argument('--protocol', action="store",
dest="protocol", default='tcp')
  parser.add_argument('--src-ip', action="store", dest="src_ip",
default='1.1.1.1')
  parser.add_argument('--src-port', action="store",
dest="src_port", default=randint(0, 65535))
  parser.add_argument('--dst-ip', action="store", dest="dst_ip",
default='192.168.1.51')
  parser.add_argument('--dst-port', action="store",
dest="dst_port", default=randint(0, 65535))
  parser.add_argument('--flags', action="store", dest="flags",
default=None)
  # parse arguments
  given_args = parser.parse_args()
  iface, protocol, src_ip,  src_port, dst_ip, dst_port, flags =
given_args.iface, given_args.protocol, given_args.src_ip,\
  given_args.src_port, given_args.dst_ip, given_args.dst_port,
given_args.flags
  send_packet(protocol, src_ip, src_port, flags, dst_ip,
dst_port, iface)
```

In order to run this script, enter the following commands:

```
tcpdump src 192.168.1.66
tcpdump: verbose output suppressed, use -v or -vv for full protocol
decode
listening on eth0, link-type EN10MB (Ethernet), capture size 65535 bytes
^C18:37:34.309992 IP 192.168.1.66.60698 > 192.168.1.51.666: Flags [S],
seq 0, win 8192, length 0

1 packets captured
1 packets received by filter
0 packets dropped by kernel

$ sudo python 9_5_modify_ip_in_a_packet.py
WARNING: No route found for IPv6 destination :: (no default route?)
.
Sent 1 packets.
```

How it works...

This script defines a `send_packet()` function to construct the IP packet using `Scapy`. The source and destination addresses and ports are supplied to it. Depending on the protocol, for example, TCP or UDP, it constructs the correct type of packet. If the packet is TCP, the flags argument is used; if not, an exception is raised.

In order to construct a TCP packet, `Sacpy` supplies the `IP()/TCP()` function. Similarly, in order to create a UDP packet, the `IP()/UDP()` function is used.

Finally, the modified packet is sent using the `send()` function.

Replaying traffic by reading from a saved pcap file

While playing with network packets, you may need to replay traffic by reading from a previously saved `pcap` file. In that case, you'd like to read the `pcap` file and modify the source or destination IP addresses before sending them.

How to do it...

Let us use `Scapy` to read a previously saved `pcap` file. If you don't have a `pcap` file, you can use the *Saving packets in the pcap format using pcap dumper* recipe of this chapter to do that.

Then, parse the arguments from the command line and pass them to a `send_packet()` function along with the parsed raw packets.

Listing 9.6 gives the code for replaying traffic by reading from a saved `pcap` file, as follows:

```
#!/usr/bin/env python
# Python Network Programming Cookbook -- Chapter - 9
# This program is optimized for Python 2.7.
# It may run on any other version with/without modifications.

import argparse
from scapy.all import *


def send_packet(recvd_pkt, src_ip, dst_ip, count):
  """ Send modified packets"""
  pkt_cnt = 0
  p_out = []

  for p in recvd_pkt:
    pkt_cnt += 1
    new_pkt = p.payload
    new_pkt[IP].dst = dst_ip
    new_pkt[IP].src = src_ip
    del new_pkt[IP].chksum
    p_out.append(new_pkt)
    if pkt_cnt % count == 0:
      send(PacketList(p_out))
      p_out = []

  # Send rest of packet
  send(PacketList(p_out))
  print "Total packets sent: %d" %pkt_cnt

if __name__ == '__main__':
  # setup commandline arguments
  parser = argparse.ArgumentParser(description='Packet Sniffer')
  parser.add_argument('--infile', action="store", dest="infile",
default='pcap1.pcap')
  parser.add_argument('--src-ip', action="store", dest="src_ip",
default='1.1.1.1')
  parser.add_argument('--dst-ip', action="store", dest="dst_ip",
default='2.2.2.2')
  parser.add_argument('--count', action="store", dest="count",
default=100, type=int)
```

```
    # parse arguments
    given_args = ga = parser.parse_args()
    global src_ip, dst_ip
    infile, src_ip, dst_ip, count =  ga.infile, ga.src_ip,
  ga.dst_ip, ga.count
    try:
      pkt_reader = PcapReader(infile)
      send_packet(pkt_reader, src_ip, dst_ip, count)
    except IOError:
      print "Failed reading file %s contents" % infile
      sys.exit(1)
```

If you run this script, it will read the saved `pcap` file, `pcap1.pcap`, by default and send the packet after modifying the source and destination IP addresses to `1.1.1.1` and `2.2.2.2` respectively, as shown in the following output. If you use the `tcpdump` utility, you can see these packet transmissions.

```
# python 9_6_replay_traffic.py
...
Sent 3 packets.
Total packets sent 3
----
# tcpdump src 1.1.1.1
tcpdump: verbose output suppressed, use -v or -vv for full protocol
decode
listening on eth0, link-type EN10MB (Ethernet), capture size 65535
bytes
^C18:44:13.186302 IP 1.1.1.1.www > ARennes-651-1-107-2.w2-
2.abo.wanadoo.fr.39253: Flags [P.], seq 2543332484:2543332663, ack
3460668268, win 65535, length 179
1 packets captured
3 packets received by filter
0 packets dropped by kernel
```

How it works...

This recipe reads a saved `pcap` file, `pcap1.pcap`, from the disk using the `PcapReader()` function of `Scapy` that returns an iterator of packets. The command-line arguments are parsed if they are supplied. Otherwise, the default value is used as shown in the preceding output.

The command-line arguments and the packet list are passed to the `send_packet()` function. This function places the new packets in the `p_out` list and keeps track of the processed packets. In each packet, the payload is modified, thus changing the source and destination IPs. In addition to this, the `checksum` packet is deleted as it was based on the original IP address.

After processing one of the packets, it is sent over the network immediately. After that, the remaining packets are sent in one go.

Scanning the broadcast of packets

If you encounter the issue of detecting a network broadcast, this recipe is for you. We can learn how to find the information from the broadcast packets.

How to do it...

We can use `Scapy` to sniff the packets arriving to a network interface. After each packet is captured, they can be processed by a callback function to get the useful information from it.

Listing 9.7 gives the code for scanning the broadcast of packets, as follows:

```
#!/usr/bin/env python
# Python Network Programming Cookbook -- Chapter - 9
# This program is optimized for Python 2.7.
# It may run on any other version with/without modifications.


from scapy.all import *
import os
captured_data = dict()

END_PORT = 1000

def monitor_packet(pkt):
  if IP in pkt:
    if not captured_data.has_key(pkt[IP].src):
      captured_data[pkt[IP].src] = []

    if TCP in pkt:
      if pkt[TCP].sport <=  END_PORT:
        if not str(pkt[TCP].sport) in captured_data[pkt[IP].src]:
           captured_data[pkt[IP].src].append(str(pkt[TCP].sport))
```

```
    os.system('clear')
    ip_list = sorted(captured_data.keys())
    for key in ip_list:
      ports=', '.join(captured_data[key])
      if len (captured_data[key]) == 0:
        print '%s' % key
      else:
        print '%s (%s)' % (key, ports)

  if __name__ == '__main__':
    sniff(prn=monitor_packet, store=0)
```

If you run this script, you can list the broadcast traffic's source IP and ports. The following is a sample output from which the first octet of the IP is replaced:

```
# python 9_7_broadcast_scanning.py
10.0.2.15
XXX.194.41.129 (80)
XXX.194.41.134 (80)
XXX.194.41.136 (443)
XXX.194.41.140 (80)
XXX.194.67.147 (80)
XXX.194.67.94 (443)
XXX.194.67.95 (80, 443)
```

How it works...

This recipe sniffs packets in a network using the `sniff()` function of `Scapy`. It has a `monitor_packet()` callback function that does the postprocessing of packets. Depending on the protocol, for example, IP or TCP, it sorts the packets in a dictionary called `captured_data`.

If an individual IP is not already present in the dictionary, it creates a new entry; otherwise, it updates the dictionary with the port number for that specific IP. Finally, it prints the IP addresses and ports in each line.

Index

Symbols

A

B

C

D

E

F

G

H

I

Q

R

S

X

Z

Thank you for buying

Python Network Programming Cookbook

About Packt Publishing

Packt, pronounced 'packed', published its first book "*Mastering phpMyAdmin for Effective MySQL Management*" in April 2004 and subsequently continued to specialize in publishing highly focused books on specific technologies and solutions.

Our books and publications share the experiences of your fellow IT professionals in adapting and customizing today's systems, applications, and frameworks. Our solution based books give you the knowledge and power to customize the software and technologies you're using to get the job done. Packt books are more specific and less general than the IT books you have seen in the past. Our unique business model allows us to bring you more focused information, giving you more of what you need to know, and less of what you don't.

Packt is a modern, yet unique publishing company, which focuses on producing quality, cutting-edge books for communities of developers, administrators, and newbies alike. For more information, please visit our website: `www.packtpub.com`.

About Packt Open Source

In 2010, Packt launched two new brands, Packt Open Source and Packt Enterprise, in order to continue its focus on specialization. This book is part of the Packt Open Source brand, home to books published on software built around Open Source licences, and offering information to anybody from advanced developers to budding web designers. The Open Source brand also runs Packt's Open Source Royalty Scheme, by which Packt gives a royalty to each Open Source project about whose software a book is sold.

Writing for Packt

We welcome all inquiries from people who are interested in authoring. Book proposals should be sent to `author@packtpub.com`. If your book idea is still at an early stage and you would like to discuss it first before writing a formal book proposal, contact us; one of our commissioning editors will get in touch with you.

We're not just looking for published authors; if you have strong technical skills but no writing experience, our experienced editors can help you develop a writing career, or simply get some additional reward for your expertise.

[PACKT] open source
community experience distilled
PUBLISHING

Mastering Python Regular Expressions

ISBN: 978-1-78328-315-6 Paperback: 110 pages

Leverage regular expressions in Python even for the most complex features

1. Explore the workings of Regular Expressions in Python.
2. Learn all about optimizing regular expressions using RegexBuddy.
3. Full of practical and step-by-step examples, tips for performance, and solutions for performance-related problems faced by users all over the world.

Python Data Visualization Cookbook

ISBN: 978-1-78216-336-7 Paperback: 280 pages

Over 60 recipes that will enable you to learn how to create attractive visualizations using Python's most popular libraries

1. Learn how to set up an optimal Python environment for data visualization.
2. Understand the topics such as importing data for visualization and formatting data for visualization.
3. Understand the underlying data and how to use the right visualizations.

Please check **www.PacktPub.com** for information on our titles

46648474R00131

Made in the USA
Middletown, DE
05 August 2017